SPORTS DOG
NEW TRICKS

Training to sharpen performance

Richard Curtis

This book is dedicated to all my dogs I have trained over the years, and have improved my skills as a trainer.

PHOTOGRAPHY
Andrew Cartlidge, Rivergate Photography

Copyright © 2020 by Richard Curtis and First Stone Publishing

First published in 2020 by First Stone Publishing,
an imprint of Westline Publishing Limited

The Old Hen House
St Martin's Farm, Zeals
Warminster BA12 6NZ
United Kingdom.

ISBN 9781910488584

All rights reserved. No part of this book may be used or reproduced in any manner whatsoever, including electronic media or photocopying, without written permission from the publisher, except in the case of brief quotations embodied in critical reviews.

Cover and interior design: Alan Cooper

Printed by Printworks Global Ltd., London & Hong Kong

1 2 3 4 5 6 7 8 9 0

Contents

Chapter One: **Questions and Answers** — *page 5*

Chapter Two: **The Training Process** — *page 16*

Chapter Three: **For Starters** — *page 19*
Twist and whirly; Circling the handler; Hand touch;
Paws on a box; Middle; Walk back; Give a paw.

Chapter Four: **Motivational Tricks** — *page 36*
Jump through your arms; Leg weaves;
Combining twist and whirly; Figure of eight;
Jump into your arms.

Chapter Five: **Body Awareness** — *page 48*
Pirouette on a box; Take a bow; Feet in a box;
Side pass; Sit on a block; Reverse; Raise a back leg; Wave.

Chapter Six: **Core Strength, Stretching and Flexibility** — *page 68*
Stick 'em up; Sit pretty; Reverse; Say your prayers;
Popping from down to bow; Roll-over.

Chapter Seven: **Focus and Thinking** — *page 82*
Distance back up; Look left and right (basic, advanced);
Head in cone; Big circle around objects; Go hide; Play dead.

Chapter Eight: **Low Impact Tricks** — *page 102*
Feet on feet; Wrap a leg around a cane;
Removing cards from slots; Close a drawer;
Flip and through a hoop; Nodding dog; Dig.

Summary — *page 119*

Chapter 1: Getting Started

Trick training is fun, and when a dog has learnt through positive reinforcement, he not only loves showcasing his skills, but also enjoys the training journey. However there are additional benefits, which are widely recognised within the dog training fraternity. Many of the positive outcomes from trick training apply to pet dogs, but, in this book, I am focusing on the tricks that are of specific value to sports and performance dogs. It goes without staying that heelwork to music and canine freestyle enthusiasts will find them of use. But, increasingly, handlers from other disciplines, most particularly agility and obedience, see trick training as integral to the development of competition dogs.

The work involved in learning, and performing, tricks develops:

Physical capabilities: Many of the tricks require core strength, co-ordination, balance and flexibility. This not only keeps the dog at peak physical fitness, but also develops skills which may well cross over to your chosen discipline.

Mental flexibility: Tricks range from relatively simple to highly complex, but the process of learning involves focus, engagement, processing, problem solving and initiative – all-important in developing a dog's brainpower!

Motivation: Many tricks, such as *jump into your arms* (see page 45) are fun to perform, and can, therefore, be used as a means of motivating a dog that lacks enthusiasm. If you add a fun move before, or after, an exercise, it will increase drive and also encourage a more positive attitude.

Control: A high-drive dog can be hard to control, particularly when he can self-reward by throwing himself at the task in hand, with scant regard for your instructions. However, if you ask a dog of this kind to perform a trick on the start-line, or before a particular exercise, you can focus his attention so that he is ready to engage with you.

Relationships: To build a successful partnership you need a dog that loves working with you; a dog that finds training a stimulating, rewarding and enriching experience. If you are teaching your dog to perform in any dog sport, you cannot spend the entire time training the required exercises as he will quickly get bored and lose motivation. Teaching tricks not only varies the training schedule but, as a handler, you are more likely to adopt a light-hearted approach, thus improving your relationship with your dog.

In addition, there may be times when you cannot train specifically for your chosen sport. Your dog may be recovering from injury or surgery, the weather may be too bad to train outside or, in the winter, it is may be too dark. Faced with any of these scenarios, trick training provides the perfect solution, keeping your dog both mentally and physically exercised.

When a trick is performed well, it looks easy. But, as with all types of training, the handler needs to work hard to build strong foundations to establish learning, and to ensure that the dog is always a happy and willing partner. To help you get started, I have listed the questions that I am most commonly asked and, hopefully, my answers will give you a good overview of trick training, and how to go about it.

Do I need to use a clicker to teach tricks?

A clicker is a great tool for teaching a dog to perform a trick, particularly in the initial stages. If you mark the behaviour you want, and then reward it, the dog quickly learns that this is what you want – and what gets rewarded gets repeated.

The downside of using a clicker is that often a handler will click and feed the dog, but fail to interact verbally. If you use a clicker, don't be afraid to praise your dog after you have marked his behaviour, as this will keep him interested and engaged.

Many of the tricks, outlined in this book, can be taught without using a clicker, especially if you have a clicker word such as "yes" to mark the behaviour you want.

If you are using a clicker word, be careful not to overuse it; your clicker word – "yes" – should be doing the same job as the 'click'. If you feel that your delivery is inconsistent, it may be better to opt for a vocal sound, such as a 'click' or a 'clock', which will be more uniform.

Can you teach young dogs to perform tricks?

Yes, you can teach puppies and young dogs some of the tricks featured in this book, but you must ensure that a youngster does not repeat them too often. Frequent repetition can put undue strain on a vulnerable growing body, so moderation is key.

You also need to be selective about the tricks you teach, so that their physical impact is minimal. You need to opt for tricks where the dog is balanced, rather than those that require him to lean over to one side, or where he needs to jump or race at speed, as this is when injuries are more likely to happen.

I have outlined a number of tricks that are suitable for youngsters in *Chapter Eight: Low Impact Tricks*.

Are any moves suitable for dogs rehabilitating from injuries or for older dogs to learn?

Canine physiotherapists are now making wide use of tricks as an aid to recovery from injury and as a means of rehabilitation. Obviously the choice of trick taught will depend on the injury sustained and it may be that physical exertion must be kept to a minimum. For this reason I have included some very simple tricks in this book, such as *head in a cone* (see page 90) and *look left and right* (see page 85) which require little movement, and may, therefore, be suitable for dogs that have significant issues with mobility. Before starting any training, check with your vet or canine physiotherapist to ensure it is suitable for your dog.

An older dog can be taught a variety of tricks but, as with a youngster, you need to think about what you are asking him to do. An older dog will not be as strong, as quick in his movement, or as flexible, as an adult in his prime. In this case, you should focus on static tricks – for example, *wrap a leg around a cane* (see page 105) and *removing cards from slots* (see page 108).

What rewards should I use?

Go for any reward your dog truly values so he is in no doubt that his efforts have been worthwhile! A food reward is probably the easiest to work with, particularly when you first start trick training.

Food rewards can be divided into categories:

Low value: This could be pieces of kibble, which the dog might get as part of its daily food ration. If you have a food-mad dog that slobbers at the mere sight of food, or tries to mug your hand for any sign of food, then this lower value type reward might work best, particularly in the initial stages of training. Sometimes a dog who is food mad cannot think when the handler has more interesting treats, so starting with more boring food can help to keep him calmer and, therefore, more able to process instructions.

Medium value: The type of food might include proprietary dog treats, such as meaty sticks. These are more interesting to the dog and will encourage him to repeat the behaviour in expectation of this slightly higher value treat.

High value: The foods in this category include fresh cooked chicken, garlic sausage, cheese or liver cake. These are strong smelling and super tasty. Your dog will give you his undivided attention and will put in extra effort to earn this type of reward.

Make sure you vary the type of reward you use during a session in order to keep your dog's interest. Monitor his reaction to a various food rewards. If he is getting over-excited when he is given a particular food treat – liver cake, for example – it might be better to restrict its use and only bring it out in more challenging situations. This might be if you are asking your dog to perform a trick in a new location, or at a specific time.

Toy rewards are another great tool for the trick trainer as the dog is not only interacting with you while you are teaching the trick but also while you are rewarding him – playing tug, for example. From a young age, you need to teach the dog that the best game with a toy is when he is playing with you. I do this by working with two toys of equal value.

First, I play with toy one and let the dog have it. I then produce toy two and make it come alive so that the dog leaves toy one in order to engage with the toy that I am playing with.

Initially, your dog may be reluctant to leave toy one, which is in his possession. You must, therefore, make toy two more exciting, activating it by throwing it around, juggling it, dragging it along the floor or just pretending to talk to the toy as if it's something really interesting.

In the early stages this might be a struggle but, if you persist, you should find the dog releases 'his' toy in favour of 'your' toy. When this happens, and your dog engages with the toy, go wild with praise and excitement so he is in no doubt he has made the right choice. Don't worry about asking him to release his new-found toy; let him win the game! While he is celebrating, retrieve toy one and then repeat the game.

In the same way as when you are using food rewards, vary the type of toy – and its perceived value – to keep training motivational and interesting.

Can I use my dog's daily food ration as rewards?

Yes, your dog's daily food ration is a very useful source of training rewards. The benefit of using his food is that he is not having extra rewards on top of his daily dinner so his weight will be kept in check. The other advantage is that you can use it piecemeal during training, or you can give a jackpot reward, giving your dog big handfuls if he makes a breakthrough or does something particularly well.

How should the food rewards be deployed during a training session?

Keeping the deployment of the rewards unpredictable helps to keep a dog focused and motivated. Often, handlers simply reward from the hand, which is fine for some dogs. However, this can easily become boring and predictable so you may need to up your game by making the treats come alive.

Here are a few different ways of giving food rewards:

Chase the rabbit: With the food in your hand, get the dog to chase after it as you move away, or turn around in a circle

Running rabbit: Throw the reward along the ground – the further you throw the reward, the more the dog will enjoy the chase.

Catch it: Throw the treat towards the dog so that he can catch it. You may need to teach your dog to catch a treat first as some do not do it naturally:

- Move your hand very slowly a few times, as if to throw, before launching it at the dog. This will give him a chance to see the rhythm.
- Position the dog further away from you so he will be able to see the reward coming towards him for longer, thus giving him a chance to follow it and time a catch.

Flying bird: Place the reward on the back of one of your hand and use your fingers, on the other hand, to flick it towards the dog. The 'flight' will be unpredictable, particularly if your flicking isn't that good!

Dive bomber: Throw the treat up high so that it drops from a great height – the dog can either chase it or catch it.

Machine gun: This technique is not so much about deploying the treat but more about the amount of treats that you give the dog. Rewarding the dog with one food treat each time can become a bit boring so multiple feeding of small rewards provides added excitement.

What reward rate should I employ during a training session?

In the initial stages of teaching a trick, you should use a high rate of reinforcement when the dog is learning the first element. This will help to engage him and encourage him to make an effort. When you have got past the first few training sessions, you might start to reward on a more random basis, varying the number and type of rewards you are using.

Bear in mind, you may whizz through some stages quickly, but others may take longer. If your dog is struggling, go back to a much higher rate of reward for performing a smaller element of the trick.

What sort of attitude should I be looking for?

Trick training is all about having fun so your dog should be alert and interested with ears up, eyes bright and with a wagging tail, regardless of what you are teaching him. All of these traits can be affected by the handler's attitude. If you fail to be enthusiastic and energetic, you dog will pick up on it and this will influence his mood.

Why not try making a big fuss of him, or run around with him before you start training in order to put him in a happy, positive mind-set?

If you are not seeing upbeat behaviour in your dog, you need to examine what you might be doing wrong. Ask yourself the following questions:

- Have I been using the same food reward for too long?
- Am I persisting with a trick, even though the dog needs a break from it?
- Does the dog need more variety in the type of food/toy rewards I am providing?
- Were my expectations in a session too high? Did I put too much pressure on the dog?
- Have I tried to move through the stages of a trick too quickly and confused the dog?
- Am I over-practising a trick?

There are times when it's advisable to back off from training a particular trick if it's not going right. I have often found that time off from a trick can result in a better attitude when you go back to it.

What should I do if my dog is getting confused between two moves?

When you start teaching a new trick, it may be that your dog decides that he wants to do a different trick, which he has already learnt. If you see signs of this, you will need to strip back the new trick and ask for a smaller element. This allows you to reward the dog quicker so he doesn't have a chance to perform his 'preferred' trick. You can then progress slowly, so the dog sees that the new trick is as rewarding as the old one due to the high rate of reward.

Confusion over moves is also caused if verbal cues are too similar. You need to ensure that the cue you use for a new trick is distinctive and bears no relation to any of the other commands in your dog's repertoire. Remember, it doesn't matter what the cues mean to you, as long as they sound different, so you could use 'banana', 'orange' and 'lemon' as cues, as these three words all sound different.

It can also be confusing if the tricks you are teaching all start in the same position. For example, moves such as *sit pretty* (see page 71), *reverse* (see page 59) and *give a paw* (see page 33), all start with the dog in a sit. To avoid confusion, select just of these tricks to teach in a session. Make sure that one trick is well progressed before attempting another trick that might be deemed to be similar.

What should I do if my dog gets over-excited, or is barking, when I am teaching him a trick?

Some people might say a dog getting excited about learning is not a bad thing but, sometimes, a dog getting too excited about a trick can be detrimental and injurious to the dog. For example, if a dog is too enthusiastic about performing a *roll-over* (see page 78), he could throw himself to the floor, hurting his shoulder in the process.

If this over-the-top energy is creeping into a trick, try to instil some control as the dog is performing the trick. So if he is getting excited during a leg weave, ask him to go under a leg and lie down, then count to five before rewarding him in the down. Repeat for the following weave so the dog has a chance to chill before he gets a reward.

Some dogs are naturally very excitable; with this type of dog you need to be calm and clear about what you require. Quiet praise and rewarding lower category rewards help to decrease the dog's exuberance

What role does a handler's voice play in terms of a reward?

Your voice can really help to convey that what your dog has just done is amazing! With a higher drive dog you can click, or use your clicker word, so he knows he is doing as you ask, but with many dogs this is not sufficiently motivating.

So, when you have marked the behaviour you want, and rewarded with food/toy, try to keep the attitude and energy going by engaging the dog with your voice. The higher the tones of voice you can use with a low drive dog, the better. If he is still not as engaged as you would like, try dancing a little jig and cheer him when he has done something right. Your neighbours might think you are mad – but your dog will be enthused!

Try not to get into the "good dog" vocal praise mentality as this gets very boring. When praising the dog try to use words where your vocal pitch changes; words such as "great", "wow" and "super" sound far more exciting. Short words, like "yes", grab the dog's attention, but don't be afraid to have a conversation with him. This will help to keep him engaged while you are working, as many dogs will switch off as soon as they have received the reward.

Above all, stay positive with your voice, and make sure you don't start to use negative words. When a dog is failing to achieve part of a move, the handler can, unknowingly, keep saying "ahh" or "no" which starts to have a negative impact on the dog's attitude to a training session. Some dogs even react to a handler's facial expression; a frown of concentration, or a glare, can be very unsettling. So, no matter what's happening, try to keep a smile on your face as this conveys to the dog that you are enjoying the session as well.

How many times a day should I practise tricks?

The amount of practice you do will depend on your dog, and the stage of training you have reached in relation to a particular trick. Brief sessions of no more than five minutes are always best in order to maintain the dog's focus and enthusiasm.

When you start to train a trick the dog is often very enthusiastic, as the reward rate is high. He will, therefore, be happy to perform the starting element of the trick many times. If the trick is in the refining, or extending, phase, you may want to limit the number of repetitions to about three, with specific goals in mind:

First rep: Review what you did on the last session.

Second rep: Make an improvement.

Third rep: Drop back to what you did for the first rep, to give the dog confidence that what he did on the second rep was correct, but he is not under pressure.

As dog trainers we do tend to suffer from the 'just one more go' syndrome, which can ruin a training session if the last repetition doesn't go right. So always try to leave a trick on an improvement and move on to a different trick, perhaps coming back to the first trick later in the training session.

When practising tricks it is best to have two or three in mind, so you can switch between them during the training session to add variety. The tricks that you teach in that session should be very different: *leg weaves* (see page 39), *sit pretty* (see page 71), and *head in a cone* (see page 90), for example. These three tricks should not interfere with each other, and will not add confusion to your training session. In contrast, teaching the dog to *reverse* (see page 59), and to *look left and right* (see page 85) will be highly confusing, as these two tricks require the handler to be positioned behind the dog.

The number of training sessions a day could be around three, as long as they are restricted to five minutes per session. However, you need to keep monitoring your dog's attitude and making sure that he is enjoying the work. Days off can sometimes have more benefit than constantly training a trick.

When planning a session, first consider if your dog is in the right mood for training. Each dog is different; some need to be energised, so perhaps train this type of dog before he goes for a walk or has his meal. With a higher drive dog, it might be better to train it at the end of the day after he has had some exercise, so that his brain is more able to process information.

What is proofing a trick?

When you are working on a trick, you might have done all the training in the same room in the house. This means the dog gets conditioned to performing the trick in that place, and with you positioned in exactly the same place. Proofing involves getting the dog to perform the trick no matter where he is, what is going on around him, and regardless of what you are doing.

It's easy to think you have trained a trick but you are probably unaware that you have always stood in a certain way and held your hands in the same place. So the first way of proofing a trick is to start moving your arms and legs. You might not be able to do this with every trick, but many of them will allow you to move at least one arm.

Test your dog by asking him to do the trick while you have your arms outstretched or on your head. Now try with your hands behind your back – this will really test if the dog knows the action on a verbal cue, and not because you have given him a small body signal. If you want to make it harder, try juggling a toy while asking him to do a trick. This will really be a test but, as with everything in training, start off slowly. Move the toy very slightly and gradually increase the movement, building on your dog's success.

When you ask your dog to perform a trick in a different environment, he is starting to learn that he must react to your commands no matter what is going on around him. Again, be careful about putting him in the deep end too soon. So you might start by taking the dog into the garden if the trick has been taught in the house.

When he has been successful in the garden, you might try it out in the local park when it is quiet. Even though your dog has a full understanding of the trick, and has performed it many times at home, always be prepared to drop back a few steps in training if he is struggling to perform the full trick in a new environment. It's much better for the dog to perform the trick, with some help, in a new place rather than notching up several failed attempts. Take it slowly and, as the dog's confidence grows, ask him to perform his repertoire in a variety of new places, and with increasing levels of distraction.

How can I advance my dog's tricks?

Over a period of time you may have taught your dog an extensive repertoire of tricks. The variety will help to keep his interest but, sometimes, rather than teaching a new move you can advance the tricks the dog already knows.

Here are a few ways you can progress tricks, although they may not all be applicable to the tricks you have trained:

Distance

If your dog is performing a static move: *take a bow* (see page 51) or *sit pretty* (see page 71), for example, you can ask for the move but position yourself further away from him.

When you are starting distance work, it is a good idea to sit the dog on a platform as this prevents him from coming forward, which, therefore, increases his chance of being successful. When your first start to use a platform, you will need to teach the dog to go to, and stay on, the platform – no matter where you are.

Another way of teaching your dog to perform tricks at a distance is to put him behind a physical barrier such as a baby gate, or position him on the top step of a flight of stairs which will, again, stop him coming forward.

Holding an object

Teaching the dog to hold an object can be connected to many types of tricks. Performing a simple trick such as a twist, while holding an object, makes it twice as hard, as the dog is doing two behaviours in one trick.

Sequencing tricks together

Adding tricks together can make it more testing as the dog will have to listen carefully to his verbal cues. Initially, pick tricks that flow together. If the sequence involves an acute change of direction, the dog may be physically incapable of performing these tricks in succession.

Single command

There are some tricks where you can give a single command, and the dog will perform the move multiple times. For example, when training *leg weaves (*see page 39*)*. you would start by asking the dog to "weave" every time you moved your leg forward. You can progress this by asking him to "weave", but then use the body signal of your leg coming forward as the cue for the dog to continue until told otherwise. To train this, start by giving your verbal cue, and then stay quiet but use your hand to signal that you want another leg weave – then reward. In this way the dog will understand that he must continue to weave, without verbal prompts.

How do you invent new dog tricks that are personal to your dog?

There are a variety of standard dog tricks that have been taught to dogs for many years. There are many others, which, simply due to the dog's size or personality, should not be attempted. To add to your repertoire, you should constantly look for indications of tricks which are going to suit your own, individual dog. For example, if your dog goes to sleep on his back, it will be easy to teach the *play dead* trick (see page 99). Making these observations during daily life is key to inventing new tricks to work on.

Capturing a behaviour is a great way of creating a new trick. For example, your dog may, unknowingly, sneeze when he is excited. This provides the opportunity to mark the sneeze with a click, or with your clicker word. Gradually, as the dog gets rewarded for the behaviour, he will offer it more often and so, in time, you will be able to get it on command.

When you are working with your dog, you will find that he has a particular preference for certain types of tricks so you can use this as the basis for inventing new tricks for him to perform. For example if your dog likes to tug when playing, why not teach him to pull a sock from your foot? Use your imagination, and your dog's natural skills and behaviours – and the the sky's the limit!

Chapter 2: The Training Process

No matter what trick you have decided to teach your dog, there are a number of stages which you need to go through before you arrive at the end goal of the dog performing the trick on cue.

Some of these stages will not take long to complete but others will feel like they are taking forever. This is normal as, getting the dog to perform duration or distance in a move, for example, cannot be achieved until he has fully grasped the foundations of the move.

These are the seven stages I work through when teaching a trick:

STAGE ONE

Introducing the trick normally involves some sort of luring – getting the dog to follow a treat in the desired direction, or encouraging him to move to a location as a reward is going to be given there. If the reward is in your hand, you might want to hold it in a fist rather than in your fingers. The fact that the dog cannot see the food means he will think a little more about what he is doing rather than just grabbing the food.

Some dogs prefer to work things out for themselves so you might employ shaping rather than luring. Shaping is a training method where you wait for the dog to offer a behaviour, and then mark it, rather than luring the desired behaviour. So, for instance, you might want your dog to place his paws on a box. You could lure him into position with a treat but some dogs get over-excited, or food-obsessed, and fail to process what you are asking for. In this case, you could shape the dog by standing back and marking with a click, or your clicker word, when he gets near the box. He might then sniff the box, which you would mark, as any movement near the box is going to get a reward. Gradually the dog will start to realise that being near the box gets rewards, so he will start to experiment by offering other behaviours, such as touching it with a paw.

Shaping takes patience, and good timing, as you need to mark the exact behaviour you want at the precise moment the dog is doing it. If you use this method of training you need to be careful that the dog doesn't get frustrated, as this can easily result in him barking or simply switching off. As with all training sessions, keep them short and don't expect big leaps in the progression of the trick at every session.

STAGE TWO

At this stage the dog should be performing the movement you require, consistently, with the aid of a hand signal. You can now introduce a verbal cue. Try not to use the command until the dog has gone past point where the move could go wrong. If you say it before the dog has performed the move correctly, he might not complete it, thus learning the wrong response to the command. At this stage of training, it is much better to give your verbal cue just as the dog is ending the correct move, rather than earlier, as there is more chance he will have completed the exact movement your require.

STAGE THREE

This involves getting rid of the food in your hand. However, you would use the empty hand to encourage the dog to perform the move, just as when you were luring him. Use an open hand to guide the dog, then reward him from the other hand, as this will help you to remove the guiding hand later on.

STAGE FOUR

This involves phasing out the guiding hand, or body signal, which prompts the move. To do this, simply reduce your physical cue so that it is far less obvious. Imagine a big rubber band around your arms, which prevents you moving them them out so far. Now think of a restriction round your hands, reducing how far you can move them.

It's very easy to get stuck at this stage, as the dog is probably performing the trick you require. However, teaching tricks is about keeping the dog's brain stimulated and making him think. If you reduce your physical cues, your dog is not relying on you – he has to work things out for himself.

STAGE FIVE

Your dog should now be able to perform the trick on a vocal command, without the help of physical signals, in order to earn his reward. It is important to check that he can perform the move when you show him that you are not holding a reward in your hand, as holding a reward can become the key to performing some tricks.

STAGE SIX

This stage involves giving the dog more to think about while he performs the trick. This might be asking for the trick while you hold your arms out to the side, or on top of your head. It's amazing how you often think your dog fully understands a verbal cue but when you do something different he becomes confused. This is often because, during training, you have always stood in exactly the same way – with your hands close to you. When this familiar picture changes, the dog loses confidence. You, therefore, need to reinforce his learning so that he can perform the trick, on a verbal cue, in all situations. Try sitting on the floor when you give your cue or, to make it even harder, place your hands on the floor as you give the command. Dogs often associate treats with hands, so your dog can easily become obsessed with looking down at your hands rather than performing the trick.

STAGE SEVEN

Advancing a trick that your dog enjoys is a great way to keep him thinking. If it is a static move, such as a *sit pretty* (see page 71), you can ask him to perform it while it is at a distance from you. If it is a moving trick, such as *leg weaves* (see page 39), you might ask for more repetitions of the trick so, for example, eight leg weaves. Putting various tricks together in a sequence is another way of advancing your dog's trick training so you might ask him to *twist* (see page 19) then do six *leg weaves*, ending with *jump through your arms* (see page 36).

Chapter 3

For starters

If you, and your dog, are new to trick training, you want to start with some moves that are relatively straightforward and highly achievable so you both feel enthused!

The starter tricks I have chosen are suitable for dogs of all ages, including youngsters, but, as with all aspects of training and physical exertion, excessive repetition should be avoided. Remember to maintain your dog's focus in training sessions by working on one trick for a few reps and then moving on to a different skill. You can always revisit the first trick later in the session, but variety prevents the dog losing interest because he has been asked for too many repetitions.

At this early stage in your dog's training it is important that you adhere closely to training process I have outlined (*see Chapter Two*) which will establish learning in achievable stages. Your dog is starting out on his trick training journey so you must also keep an eye on his attitude. You want him to enjoy his training sessions and to look forward to trick training in the future.

If a trick is not going well, take a step back and analyse what you need to do. Never be afraid to return to an earlier, easier stage. This will give you the opportunity to reward your dog, and reignite his enthusiasm – and you will both be in a better frame of mind when you are ready to increase the challenge.

TWIST AND WHIRLY

The trick

This trick is where the dog turns clockwise or anti-clockwise as if chasing his tail. It's a good trick to get the dog bending his body around which will improve his overall flexibility. In agility, a dog needs to learn his directionals – whether he should turn left or right – and this is a great way of teaching him.

Start with one direction only and when the dog has mastered that direction, you can begin training the opposite way. I use "whirly" as my clockwise command; my anti-clockwise command is "twist". Of course, you can choose your own verbal cues.

The dog spins in a clockwise and anti-clockwise direction.

▶ **Step 1:** To teach an anti-clockwise turn, start with the dog facing you, and a treat in your left hand.

▶ **Step 2:** Position the treat so it is right on the dog's nose, with his head level. Now move the treat in an anti-clockwise direction with the dog following it. Sometimes the dog may only go part of the way; this is quite common so reward him for just doing part of the turn. When he realises it's rewarding to perform part of the turn, you can ask him for a little bit more so that, eventually, he is spinning all the way around.

Start with the dog facing you; a treat in your left hand.

Turning anti-clockwise: Hold a treat on the dog's nose and lure him so that he follows the food and turns in an anti-clockwise direction.

▶ **Step 3:** When the dog is fluently following the food around, you can name the movement – I use the verbal cue, "twist" for turning anti-clockwise. Remember to name the trick when the dog clearly understands what he has to do and is performing all, or most of, the move. So, in this case, introduce the verbal cue when the dog has spun three-quarters of the way round. You can then pretty much guarantee that you will be naming the correct action.

While the dog is learning, you may need to reward partway round.

Reward when he completes the anti-clockwise spin.

▶ **Step 4:** When you feel that your dog knows the cue for the action, you can move on to the next stage of training. This is where you ask your dog to "twist" without

For starters

Fade the lure by signalling with your left hand... ...and rewarding with your right hand.

the lure of food. To do this you need to use your left hand to signal the twist, give the verbal cue, and then reward the dog from the right hand. Make sure you reward when his head is level. If you reward when his head is raised, he may not perform a clean twist with four feet on the ground. Rewarding from your right hand should mean that the dog will start performing the move to get the reward rather than just following the lure hand.

▶ **Step 5:** Now you need to decrease the hand signal. Gradually start to keep your arms closer to your body until you are not moving them at all. Your aim is to give no physical signal; the dog must rely solely on the vocal cue to perform the move.

▶ **Step 6:** When the dog can do a twist on a verbal cue, you can start training him to spin in the opposite direction, i.e. clockwise and responding to the verbal cue, "whirly". Repeat all the stages outlined above, but this time use your right hand to lure the dog and reward from your left hand.

▶ **Step 7:** After some practice, your dog will be able to perform both twist and whirly on verbal cues. You are now ready to extend his training using these moves.

Here are a few ideas:

- Ask the dog to perform twist/whirly from a sit or down position.

- Position the dog on a platform or behind a gate and ask for a twist/whirly while you step further away from him. This will result in a long-distance spin.

- Ask the dog to twist when he walking beside you in the heelwork position on your left side.

The aim is to complete the move solely on a verbal cue –in this case, "twist".

CIRCLING THE HANDLER

The trick

Turning a circle – both clockwise and anti-clockwise – around the handler.

This is an easy move for a dog to learn, no matter his age. It involves turning in a tight circle around the handler and, like twist and whirly, it is helps to improve flexibility. You should teach your dog to do both clockwise and anti-clockwise circles so that he remains physically balanced, but you will need to put them on separate verbal cues. I use "round" as my clockwise command; my anti-clockwise command is "oppo".

It's best to teach one direction and only start work on the other when the first direction is past the beginner stage.

▶ **Step 1:** Stand with your feet together and have treats in both hands. Lure the dog around you clockwise, rewarding the dog at random places on the circle.

The start position.

With a treat in your right hand, lure the dog around your body.

Reward at random intervals around the circle.

As the dog goes behind your back, use your left hand to encourage him to complete the circle.

▶ **Step 2:** After many repetitions the dog should start to follow your hands around the circle, and this is when you can start to introduce the verbal cue, "round". If your dog is toy motivated you can use a toy to guide him around you. However, chasing after the toy can mean the dog is not thinking about what he is doing, so it may be better to start with food so that he processes your instructions.

▶ **Step 3:** Now it's time to phase out the food. Use your right hand – without food – to indicate a clockwise circle. If the dog completes a clockwise circle around you, use your left hand to reward him. This should mean that the dog starts to perform the move to get the reward rather than simply following the food in the right lure-hand.

Now use your right hand to signal the clockwise direction around your body, and reward from your left hand.

▶ **Step 4:** Start to decrease the movement of your right hand until the dog goes around solely on a vocal command. Make sure you deploy the reward in different ways in order to keep the dog's drive through the move. If you are using food you could throw the food forward, or you could run forward, with the dog chasing you, after he has completed one and a half rotations of your body.

▶ **Step 5:** When you have the clockwise circle on a verbal cue, you can start training the opposite direction. The training is exactly the same, but this time you are using your left hand to signal an anti-clockwise circle, and rewarding with the right hand.

▶ **Step 6:** When the dog is confidently running around you there are various ways in which you can progress the trick:

- Try asking the dog to circle while you are sitting on a chair or on the floor. To really test your dog try sitting on the floor, with your hands underneath you, and ask him to go "round". We often use body language unconsciously so this is a way of testing if your dog really does know the command.

Once the have the clockwise circle on a verbal cue, you can teach the dog to circle in the opposite direction.

Progression

Ask for it when you are sitting in a chair or on the floor/ground.

- Ask the dog to circle you and, while he goes around you, turn the opposite way to the dog.

- Link this move with a twist so the dog performs an anti-clockwise spin then goes around you clockwise, thus performing a figure of eight.

HAND TOUCH

The trick

This trick has many uses as it gives you a means of connecting with your dog. For example:

- If you are having recall problems, asking for a *hand touch* as the dog comes in to you prevents the issue from becoming confrontational.

- If you are training an agility dog a *hand touch*, which re-establishes contact, can be used to calm a high-drive dog, or reassure an anxious dog.

- Developing the *hand touch* so that it is a moving target, which your dog can touch multiple times, is a great way to energise him.

The dog targets your hand with his nose.

In addition, a *hand touch* can be progressed to nose-touching a target, which will be required when training other tricks such as *close a drawer* (see page 110). Target training also comes in handy if you plan to train stop contacts in agility, which involves using a touch disc.

▶ **Step 1:** For this stage all you need is your hand and some tasty treats. Start by holding a treat between a couple of fingers, so the palm of your hand is flat. The dog should sniff your hand and, at that point, you should mark his response with a click, or with your clicker word, and feed him with a treat from your other hand. The reason for rewarding from the other hand is so that the dog learns that he has to touch the hand to get a reward, and not just eat a treat where he has found it.

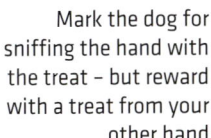

Mark the dog for sniffing the hand with the treat – but reward with a treat from your other hand

Hold a high-value treat between a couple of fingers.

▶ **Step 2:** After a few practices, remove the food from your target hand. If you keep the food in place for too long, the dog may start to nibble rather than use his nose. To establish learning, you may need to mix between food, and no food, over a period of days. You should then find that the dog starts to touch your hand with his nose in order to get the food from the other hand. When this behaviour is reliable, add the verbal cue, "touch".

▶ **Step 3:** Ask for "touch" and when the dog has placed his nose in the correct position, move your target hand and ask him to "touch" again before rewarding. Don't be afraid to move around the room, asking for quick touches in succession. However, you should remember to build in rewards for single nose touching as well to maintain motivation.

▶ **Step 4:** Up to this stage you may have been using the same hand, so now you need to make sure the dog will nose touch whichever hand is presented. Start this by asking for a touch on the right hand, then remove it to behind your back while holding out the left hand for the dog to touch.

▶ **Step 5:** Building duration on this trick is a skill which requires time and patience. To do this, ask the dog to touch but rather than rewarding a single nose touch, say nothing. The dog should touch again. If this happens, reward heavily. In this way, the dog starts to realise that he must keep his nose near the target hand and try again. Over time the dog will learn to maintain position, holding his nose on the target hand until you give him a click or use your clicker word. Make sure you are still putting in some one-touch winners so that the dog keeps motivated and puts in extra effort.

▶ **Step 6:** To advance this trick, teach the dog to maintain the nose touch while you are moving. To do this you will need to have good duration on the nose touch.

Now present your hand without a treat.

Move around asking for lots of quick touches.

Progression

Work on maintaining a hand touch on the move.

PAWS ON A BOX

The trick

This trick, which promotes balance and co-ordination, is an easy move for dogs of any age as the box, or the object you choose, can be very low to start with. Make sure the object that you are using is 100 per cent stable and, if you are working on carpet or tiles, ensure the object is not going to slide along the floor when the dog puts his feet on it.

The dog positions his front paws on a box.

▶ **Step 1:** Hold a treat in your fist, positioned above the box/object; this should encourage the dog to come forward and place a front paw on it. The moment he does this, open your fist and reward with the treat. Initially reward for one paw on the box; don't hold out for both paws – particularly if your dog is worried – as he may lose confidence quickly.

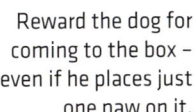

The start position.

Reward the dog for coming to the box – even if he places just one paw on it.

▶ **Step 2:** After a few successes with one paw, you can wait until the dog puts both front paws on the box before rewarding. As he gets used to where the food is, and is happy placing his paws on the box, you can introduce the verbal command "on" when both paws are on the box.

▶ **Step 3:** Pause before opening your hand to reward the dog as this will gradually build duration for standing with his front paws on the box. Remember, the dog should be randomly rewarded for holding the position for different lengths of

When he is reliably placing his two front paws on the box, introduce your verbal cue.

time rather than asking for an increase in duration each go. You can now phase out the food, still positioning your hand above the box, but rewarding with a treat from the other hand.

Fade out the lure, and reward with a treat from your other hand.

▶ **Step 4:** When the dog is connecting the command to the action, start holding your hand higher and closer to you so that he starts to go to the box without a hand signal. Try to get to the stage where the dog will go on the box, on a verbal cue, while you hold your hands behind your back.

▶ **Step 5:** Up until now you will have been standing right by the box so now start to move away and let the dog go forward to stand on it. Build up the distance gradually and shorten the distance several times in

Test your verbal cue by asking for the move with your hands held behind your back.

a training session so it doesn't keep getting harder. To stop the dog anticipating getting off the box, always return to him and reward him on the box.

▶ **Step 6:** At this stage the dog should be consistently running to the box and placing his front paws on it, on a verbal cue, so you can now advance the trick.

Here are a few options:

- When the dog is on the box extend the time period that he has to stay in position before you return to him to reward.

- Cue the dog to go on to the box and then move around while he stays in position. See if you can touch your toes, run around, or juggle a food treat while the dog stays on the box.

- When the dog is on the box, ask him to perform another trick such as *give a paw* (see page 33) or *take a bow* (see page 51).

Progression

Stand at a distance and ask for the move.

When the dog is in position, ask for an additional trick, such as *give a paw*.

MIDDLE

The trick

Many agility handlers teach this position as their start-line wait – often adding a sit or a down once the dog is in position – and obedience handlers use it to set the dog up for a sendaway. It is an easy move and is suitable for dogs of all ages.

▶ **Step 1:** Stand with the dog facing you, and your feet together. Now use a food treat to encourage the dog to go clockwise and complete a semi-circle so that he is behind you. Move your left foot away from your right (otherwise you will knock the dog with your leg) and lure him to come between your legs. Feed several treats while the dog is

The dog comes into a static position between your legs.

in this position before stepping off the dog – rather like getting off a horse. The reason for the dismount is that if you allow the dog to come out forward when you release him, he may just come through your legs, and not stop, as he deems coming out of your legs to face you is rewarding.

Starting with the dog in front of you, encourage him to turn in a clockwise direction so that he completes a semi-circle around your body.

When he gets behind you, move your left foot to create a gap.

Reward when the dog is in position.

▶ **Step 2:** Repeat step 1, introducing the verbal cue, "middle" when the dog is standing between your legs.

▶ **Step 3:** Start to signal with the right hand rather than luring the dog to go around to the middle position, and reward immediately he gets there. This is the start of removing the food lure. When you are happy the dog is achieving this, the next stage is to keep your hands higher when the dog comes into the middle position. Up until now you may have used the food to stop the dog, so now you are looking for the dog to stop of his own accord. Feed several treats when the dog gets in position and just briefly raise your hands a bit higher before dropping them down to give the dog another reward. This will acclimatise him to your hands being higher, and he will learn to remain in the middle position when your hands are not as visible.

▶ **Step 4:** So far, everything has been done without the handler moving. Now, when the dog comes into the middle position, hold the treat lower and start to move forward slowly. Make sure you are feeding several rewards as you do this and, over time, start to stand up straighter, holding your hands higher.

▶ **Step 5:** Middle is easy to combine with other moves so when your dog is proficient at gaining the position, try the following:

- Cue "middle" and when the dog is in position, ask him to *give a paw* (see page 33), *take a bow* (see page 51) or *sit pretty* (see page 71).

- When the dog is in the middle position, ask him to circle clockwise and anti-clockwise using the verbal cues you have already taught – "round" and "oppo" (see page 22) – so that he circles the relevant leg and goes back to the middle position.

Progression

Once the dog is reliably going into position, on cue, progress to moving forwards.

This is a great move for combining with other tricks, such as *give a paw*.

WALK BACK

The trick

This trick is all about the dog learning how to use his hindquarters. In agility this is a particularly useful skill as the dog needs to check his speed, and shift his weight to his hindquarters, when he goes into the weaves. He also needs back end awareness to adopt the two-on two off position which will be required when he is negotiating the seesaw, and as an option for training stop contacts on the A-frame and the dog-walk.

The dog walks backwards as you move towards him.

In this version of walk back, you are going to move towards the dog as he moves back. It is an easy move to start with a young dog but make sure you don't walk towards the dog too quickly. Take your time and allow the dog to coordinate his legs, otherwise he might 'banana' off to one side.

The start position.

By luring the dog's nose towards his chest, you will encourage him to take a step backwards.

▶ **Step 1:** Position the dog facing you and hold your hands together in front of his nose. Hold food in both hands and lure his nose down towards his chest. As the dog looks down for the food, he should make a slight backwards movement.

▶ **Step 2:** Initially, you will be rewarding for just a pace or two going backwards. You can then start to do multiples of the two small paces, making sure you reward the dog each time he has done two paces, but continuing the backwards movement rather than breaking off each time. Performing multiples in this way means that the dog is learning to back up over a longer distance but he still getting heavily rewarded to maintain his enthusiasm.

▶ **Step 3:** Introduce the "back" command as the dog is doing the trick, but watch out for that bendy body going to one side. If the back end starts to bend, turn the dog's head in the direction of the bend, and this should straighten him. However, you need to be quick to straighten his head again, otherwise he might start bending the opposite way! At this point, check your speed. Keep moving towards the dog very slowly until he is totally coordinated.

▶ **Step 4:** At this stage you should be able to stand up straighter, and take your hands away from the dog's nose. You may find that he leaps up for the food so you will have to identify the height at which you can hold your hands while still

Once the dog understands he needs to walk backwards, fade the food lure.

Test your verbal cue by eliminating all hand signals.

preventing the jump up. By now the dog should know the verbal cue and that, coupled with the physical cue of moving towards him, should result in a successful walk back.

▶ **Step 5:** Now remove your hands totally by having them behind your back and then see if you can increase the distance you both travel.

▶ **Step 6:** To advance this move you can set up the dog so he is behind you. Then start to walk backwards towards the dog while asking him to go "back". The dog should start to walk back behind you, just like he did when facing you.

Progression

Turn your back on the dog and ask him to walk back.

GIVE A PAW

The trick

This trick demands a degree of balance, but it is easy to teach and can be progressed to a more advanced stage once the dog has learnt the basic behaviour.

▶ **Step 1:** Position the dog in a sit facing you and have a treat in your left hand.

▶ **Step 2:** Using your right hand, pick up the dog's left paw, and then

The dog lifts his front paw.

The start position.

Use your right hand to pick up the dog's left paw.

feed him a treat from the left hand. Repeat this stage until you see the dog start to raise his paw to touch your hand as it to comes down towards him.

▶ **Step 3:** The dog is now anticipating that you will be picking up his paw so you can introduce the verbal cue "foot" as he makes contact with your hand.

▶ **Step 4:** Once your dog has mastered giving a paw with his left foot, you can work through the same stages, but this time use your left hand to pick up his right foot. I use the command "paw" so that it doesn't sound anything like the "foot" command. I like to introduce the foot change as soon as the dog has grasped the basics with his left foot. If you delay, the dog may become foot focused and be reluctant to give his right paw.

For starters

▶ **Step 5:** To advance this trick, raise your hand higher so the dog cannot touch it with his paw. This will teach him to lift his foot in the air and hold it there. You can use your verbal cue, which means hold up your paw until told otherwise.

Another way of advancing this trick is to work from a distance and ask the dog to raise his paw. Start close to the dog, and gradually move further away, making sure he is still responding correctly, on cue.

> **TOP TIP** *When you are working on distance, sit the dog on the top step of a flight of stairs to perform the trick, as this will prevent him coming forward.*

Progression

Increase duration so the dog holds his paw in the air until told otherwise.

Chapter 4: Motivational Moves

These tricks are performed on the move, and are fun for both dog and handler. If the dog is lower drive in his attitude, you can really go for it with these moves, giving plenty of vocal praise and encouragement, both during and after the dog has completed elements of training. In contrast, if you have a high-drive dog who is easily aroused, you may need to put in some control after the trick, such as a sit or down, before rewarding, so that you control his level of excitement.

Motivational moves are best performed after the dog has been warmed up, so make sure he has moved around at various paces before starting training. Obviously, you need to ensure your dog is fully fit, and has no injury issues, before attempting these moves.

JUMP THROUGH YOUR ARMS

The trick

If your dog is fit and active, he will love this trick! It's a great move to motivate your dog, particularly if he is low in drive, as the energy you create from the jump can be taken into the exercise you want him to perform. For example, if your dog is not overly excited about training that involves the weaves, you might ask him for a jump through the arms before and after a weave exercise. As the dog loves the trick, he should set off with a better attitude before he enters the weave. Then repeating the trick afterwards will give him an extra reward, in addition to the toy/treat reward you generally use in training.

Create a hoop shape with your arms for the dog to jump through.

As with any move which involves jumping, you must be aware of the surface you are working on as it is all too easy for the dog to slip on landing. Therefore, this move should only be performed on grass or carpet.

To teach him to jump through your arms, you will need a pole around one metre (3 ft) in length. A plastic pipe is ideal as it is light but durable; it is known as conduit and is available from hardware stores. If you require a curved pole (see step 2), a length of garden hose will suffice.

Motivational Moves

In addition, you will need some solid, visible treats, such as chunks of cheese. If your dog prefers a toy reward, you can use his favourite toy. For the purpose of this exercise I am using a tennis ball.

▶ **Step 1:** Place the dog on your left side in a sit and walk forward a couple of paces. Turn left so your left side is facing the dog. Hold the pole in your left hand and a tennis ball in your right hand. Place the end of the pole between your ankles so that you are forming a hoop using the pole and your body. Lower your left hand down until the pole is almost horizontal. Now use your right hand to encourage the dog to come forward and jump the hoop, and then throw the treat to reward him on landing. Make sure you throw the treat straight, as this will help the dog to jump in a straight line.

The start position

Encourage the dog to jump through the 'hoop'.

Throw the ball as he lands – making sure you aim straight.

TOP TIP *Stand in a doorway so the dog cannot go around either side of you. If he attempts to go underneath the pole, lower your left hand nearer to the floor.*

▶ **Step 2:** After a few training sessions, the dog should know what is expected of him, so you can gradually start to raise the end of the pole from between your ankles so that it is further up your legs. When you are doing this, check that the dog still has a big enough hoop to get through. If you feel it's getting a bit small, you can try bending your left arm, or replace the straight pole with a curved pole. When your dog is reliable with this move, introduce the verbal cue, "over".

▶ **Step 3:** The next stage is to hold each end of the pole in your hands rather than one end between your legs. To start with, let the dog see you place the reward a

Now hold both ends of the pole to create a 'hoop'. You will need to place the reward so the dog can see where it is.

little ahead of where he is going to land. Then hold both ends of the pole in your hands, and give the dog the "over" command. The dog should jump through the hoop and head for the reward that is already in position.

▶ **Step 4:** The dog will now see the shape of the hoop and will anticipate the jump. At this stage you can start to bring your hands closer together along the pole until you are holding your hands and no longer need the pole. It may take you several sessions to move your hands closer together, so don't be in a rush to dispense with the pole. If you have a large breed of dog, or short arms, you might need to create a bigger space by holding something between your hands, such as a hat or scarf, so the dog has a big enough hoop to jump through.

Work slowly until you are ready to dispense with the pole, and the placed reward.

▶ **Step 5:** The dog should now be able to jump through your arms from your left side so when you have developed his confidence, you can start to teach him to do it in the opposite direction. You may find that you need to revisit many of the steps in the training process as, to the dog, it looks like a completely different trick.

LEG WEAVES

The trick

This well-known trick is where the dog weaves through the handler's legs in a figure of eight. Dogs enjoy doing this, and a number of agility handlers use leg weaves as part of their start-line routine to get the dog motivated and focused.

Dogs that are easily aroused can get over-excited when they are learning this trick. If this is the case, you need to add an element of control by putting in a stop after a single leg weave and rewarding a calm stop in either a sit or down.

Weaving between your legs in a figure of eight.

▶ **Step 1:** Place a food treat in both hands and stand with your feet apart. Position the dog on your left hand side facing in the same direction as you.

▶ **Step 2:** Move your right hand behind you right leg, into the gap between your legs, so that the dog can clearly see the reward. Encourage him to follow the treat in front of your left leg then through your legs to the right hand-side where you reward him. Repeat this step so that the dog returns from the right side to the left side.

▶ **Step 3:** As the dog starts to learn what is required, introduce a verbal cue as he goes through your legs. I use "weave"; if you use this for your weave training in agility, you can choose something else. At this stage you might also randomise how many weaves the dog performs, so he does not always get a treat for a single weave. You can also vary how you deliver the reward. The aim is for the dog to flow smoothly through your legs, which you can facilitate by throwing the treat forwards rather than rewarding from the hand. If you dog is motivated by toys, you can replace the treat with a toy but be careful the dog doesn't get too highly aroused and start jumping up for the toy. If he gets too excited, put stops in after some leg weaves, keeping the dog still for at least four seconds before rewarding.

The dog will learn the behaviour by following the lure from left to right...

...and from right to left.

Keep practising and the dog will learn to follow hand signals rather than being lured. Eventually, you can fade the hand signals and rely on a verbal cue.

▶ **Step 4:** Now that the dog can perform the trick it needs to be tidied up. When you first start training leg weaves, you have to bend over to lure the dog – so now try to stand up straight. Next, work on gradually fading out your hand signals so that the dog is doing the weave solely on a verbal cue. When he has reached this stage you can start to walk forwards, with the dog, while he is weaving. Whenever you make this kind of change to a trick, make sure you give the dog extra help as he may lose confidence when he is asked to navigate a moving leg.

Motivational Moves

▶ **Step 5:** Leg weaves can be performed in all directions: you can move from side to side, forward and backwards. If you have mastered these variations you can extend the move by asking the dog to spin (see page 19) after each weave, or to *take a bow* (see page 51) after each single leg weave. These additions mean the dog has to listen closely to you rather than just going headlong into the weave.

Progression

Teach your dog to leg weave when you are on the move!

COMBINING TWIST AND WHIRLY

The trick

When you have achieved a spin clockwise and anti-clockwise on command (see page 19), you can start to use them in a sequence. To achieve this you will need to move from side to side along a pretend line.

▶ **Step 1:** Position the dog, in a stand, parallel to you and looking towards your right hand.

▶ **Step 2:** Move to the right a couple of paces and ask the dog to "twist" anti-clockwise – but you only want him to perform half a twist. As the dog completes a half circle, move away from him to the left.

The dog spins anti-clockwise and clockwise in a sequence.

Move to your right a couple of paces and ask for "twist" (anti-clockwise spin).

Now move off to your left.

Ask for "whirly" (clockwise spin).

▶ **Step 3:** The dog should now be moving towards your left hand so, after a few paces, ask him to "whirly" clockwise, using the left hand to signal if help is needed. Basically, the dog is performing an elongated figure of eight.

A word of caution: Make sure you move a reasonable number of paces to the side between each spin. If you perform the twist and whirly too close together, you could ruin your dog's spin, as he will anticipate going back the opposite way. Also, the bigger the dog the more distance you need to travel to the side, as this allows him to flow and to drive out between each spin.

FIGURE OF EIGHT

The trick

Performing a figure of eight around the handler and another object.

Dogs love to run and chase, so we can harness this desire by teaching the dog to perform a figure of eight around the handler and an object. To do this your dog should have already mastered *circling the handler* (see page 22), as this trick can be used to help teach the figure of eight.

First, you need an object for the dog to go around. This should be approximately the same height as the dog, and it must also be a reasonable width, with overall dimensions of half a metre (1.5.ft) square. If the object is too low the dog may run across it, rather than circling it. If the object is too narrow – a cane for example – the dog will be forced to make a very tight circle around it, which is not as good for his body.

To start this trick we will break it down into two parts: circling the handler, and circling the object. For the purposes of this exercise, I have used a box.

▶ **Step 1:** Review *circling the handler* (see page 22) where the dog responds to the verbal cue "round", and circles the handler in a clockwise direction.

▶ **Step 2:** Place the object you have chosen in front of you and position the dog on your left side. This will be the side that he moves from when he leaves you to go around the object. With a treat in your right hand, guide the dog around the object in an anti-clockwise direction. As he goes round the back of the object and starts to come towards you, turn

The start position.

your back on him and run for a few paces before rewarding him. When stopping to reward the dog after turning away, keep your arm forward – like superman – so that the dog has to move past you rather than stop behind you. Turning your back on the dog, and rewarding him for running, will help the flow of the move later on, and the dog will return to you quicker.

Use your right hand to lure the dog round the box in an anti-clockwise direction.

▶ **Step 3:** When the dog understands the direction you want him to go, switch hands and reward from the left hand. However, you should still use the right hand to cue him to go anti-clockwise around the object. This means the dog has to think about what he is doing rather than just following the food. As he goes round the back of the object, give the verbal command, "eight", as this should, hopefully, guarantee that he has circled the object rather than doubling back. Make sure you are still running away from the object to reward or, alternatively, throw the treat so it encourages the dog to run back to you quickly.

▶ **Step 4:** You should now have the dog going forward around the object on command, so the next step is to link it with circling round the handler. Start with the dog on the left, and ask him to circle you first in a clockwise direction – "round" – then ask him to circle the object anti-clockwise – "eight". Turn and run away, rewarding, as before, when the dog is past you. Now try it the opposite way: ask the dog to circle the object and then circle around you. This time you are rewarding the dog for circling the handler, so be ready with the treat when he gets back to your left-hand side. Juggling between these two sequences will help to build confidence.

Now position the dog on your left and ask him to circle you in a clockwise direction …

….before heading to circle the box anti-clockwise. Turn your back on him and reward from the left hand.

▶ **Step 5:** By now the trick should be flowing nicely with the dog performing a full figure of eight. However, you are probably still using both commands – "round" and "eight" – to instruct him. To reduce this to one command, give the verbal cue, "eight" to go around the object, then use your right hand to signal he must circle the handler. Reward when he gets back to your left side. As the dog gets used to being rewarded on your left side, after circling the object, he will naturally go around you so then the whole figure of eight trick will be performed on the one command – "eight".

▶ **Step 6:** It becomes exciting for the dog when you add speed so, having taught it close up, you are now ready to add distance so he can accelerate to and from the object. This should be done gradually, stepping further from the object, one pace at a time. Don't forget, you can still run away from the dog to give the reward, which will increase his motivation to run back faster.

JUMP INTO YOUR ARMS

The trick

As with any trick, jumping into your arms has to be taught step-by-step but, once learnt, it can become a reward in itself as dogs love performing it!

Initially, you will need to use a low stool, or chair, and you may need a blanket to place in your lap.

The dog jumps from the ground, and into your arms, on a verbal cue.

▶ **Step 1:** Position the dog in a sit, facing your left hand-side, and sit on the floor with a treat in your right hand. Using the food in your right hand, encourage the dog to place his front or back feet on the upper part of your legs. If you have a medium-sized dog, he may not be able to place all four paws on you but, if you change the height and location of the food, you might be able to get three paws.

Encourage the dog to place all four feet in your lap.

Repeat – but, this time, ask for the move when you are sitting on a low stool.

▶ **Step 2:** Now sit on a low stool and encourage the dog to come from the left, following the food towards you, and placing all four feet in your lap. If you encourage the dog to come across you, in order to accommodate his back feet, he may remove his front feet. So, when he has his front feet in position, use you left hand to scoop up his back-end so that he is standing or sitting on your lap. Make sure you have multiple treats in your right hand so that you can feed very frequently. When asking the dog to dismount, try not to let him slip off in any direction. If possible, lift him off your lap on to the floor. If the dog is too big, and you cannot lift him when sitting on the stool, try to guide him to dismount slowly to your right.

Now sit on a chair and ask the dog to jump into your lap.

▶ **Step 3:** After several repetitions of helping the dog to get on your lap, he should anticipate where the reward is going to be given, and will jump into position without assistance. However, you are asking the dog to jump on to an unstable surface, so you may need to spend many weeks helping him on to your lap. Wait until you are confident that the dog is ready to jump into your lap, without help, and then you can name the trick "jump". Make sure you give the verbal cue as the dog is jumping into your lap.

Motivational Moves 47

▶ **Step 4:** Using exactly the same technique, progress the trick by sitting on something a little higher, such as a chair. When the dog is on your lap, put your left arm around him to keep him in position while feeding from the right hand, then lift him down to the floor. You are now ready to try the trick without the chair.
To transition this move, lean back against a wall so that you have some stability. Bend your legs, as far as possible, so that you are creating the appearance of a lap, which the dog can aim for. Give your verbal cue, "jump" and be ready to catch the dog – timing is everything at this stage.

▶ **Step 5:** Once the dog has got the idea of jumping up on you when you are standing with bended legs, you can start to straighten a little. However, you need to take your dog's height into consideration; it may be that you always need to bend your knees, to some extent, so that he can jump comfortably. As you start to stand upright, you will have to catch the dog rather than allowing him jump into your lap. This requires good timing, and one bad experience might be off-putting in the long term. If you have a mishap, go back to sitting on the chair in order to boost the dog's confidence.

Now try the move standing up.

Chapter 5

Body Awareness

Many canine sports require the dog to be aware of his legs, and to fine-tune their function, in order to carry out the required task. This is obviously the case for heelwork to music dogs, who perform many tricks which require lifting, and positioning of, their legs. But this dexterity is equally important in agility, where a dog needs to weight shift going into the weaves, or to position his back feet when stopping on a seesaw, for example.

If you work on the tricks outlined in this chapter, your dog should become more aware of his rear end as well as all four legs. Some of the tricks focus on just one area of the body – either front or rear – but for the harder tricks – *side pass*, for example (see page 55) – the dog needs to use all four legs, and his body, at the same time.

Bear in mind, your dog may have limited body awareness when he starts this type of training. You will, therefore, need to progress some of the tricks slowly, and limit your goals in a single session, so that the dog is motivated next time you train together.

PIROUETTE ON A BOX

The trick

The dog balances his front paws on a box and circles it.

This trick aims to get the dog using its rear end and follows on from the starter trick, *paws on a box* (see page 27). The progression is that the dog goes from putting his paws on a box to maintaining this position while walking around the box. Before you start, make absolutely sure the box is stable, and it cannot slip on the surface you are using. If the box moves, it could have a detrimental effect on the dog's attitude, and his willingness to perform the trick.

▶ **Step 1:** Position the dog in front of you with his paws on the box and have a treat in your right hand.

▶ **Step 2:** Using the treat, turn the dog's head slightly down and around towards his left elbow. As the dog follows the food, he should move his back end in an anti-clockwise direction. When he has taken a pace, reward, then move to your right so that the dog is facing you again.

▶ **Step 3:** Continue rewarding, a small pace at a time, until the dog is moving freely around the box while you move around it as well.

The start position.

Lure him round the box, a step at a time, rewarding as you go.

▶ **Step 4:** Now the dog should be ready to pirouette around the box on his own. Following the same technique you used for step 2, turn the dog's head around to his left elbow – but this time you are going to stay still. The dog may hesitate when he has to go past you with his back end so, as he approaches, move to your left. This means the dog has gone past you but, actually, you have walked past his back end, which makes it easier for him while he is learning. Wait until you have moved past the dog's back end – then you can reward him. Moving across and behind the dog – and then rewarding him – will boost his confidence and he will learn that pivoting around the box is a rewarding experience.

Lure the dog around the box again – but this time, stand still.

▶ **Step 5:** As the dog gets more proficient at pirouetting all the way around the box, introduce the verbal command, "pivot".

▶ **Step 6:** Up to this point, you will have had the food near to the dog's nose. Now it's time to take the food out of your right hand and signal with it rather than using it as a lure. Don't forget to reward tiny moves as the dog will not have the treat to help him out.

▶ **Step 7:** Start to hold your right hand higher, thereby fading the signal, while emphasising your vocal command, "pivot".

▶ **Step 8:** When you have got to the stage where the dog is performing the pirouette on command, without a hand signal, stand further from the box while the dog is pivoting. Always go back to the dog to reward him so that he stays in position, on the box, and doesn't think he has to run to you.

▶ **Step 9:** When you have mastered an anti-clockwise pirouette, you can start work on the clockwise direction. Make sure you use a different command, such as "rotate", so that the dog doesn't get confused.

Now work on fading the food lure and using hand signals.

TAKE A BOW

The trick

There are many dogs who freely offer a bow when they are playing with another dog. It is a natural behaviour, but it is quite demanding as the dog is using both his front and rear end at the same. This is a beneficial trick to teach as it develops co-ordination and balance. It can also be used as a stretching exercise. When you are teaching this move, choose a verbal cue such as "bend" or "curtsy" as the word 'bow' sounds too similar to 'down'.

▶ **Step 1:** Position the dog parallel to you (across your body), with his head towards your right hand, which is holding a treat.

The dog goes down on his forequarters and raises his hindquarters.

The start position.

▶ **Step 2:** Place your left hand, palm face down, in front of the dog's back right leg. Then place your right hand, with the treat, on the dog's nose and take it down between his front feet, as close to his chest as you can. Your left hand is positioned to prevent the dog from lying down, so tickle him inside the right back leg. As soon as he goes into a bend, feed the food and encourage him to stand up. Make sure you keep your left hand under the dog to prevent him collapsing.

Lower the treat towards the ground, while keeping your left hand in position to prevent the dog going into a down.

TOP TIP *Reward just one second when your dog is in the correct position. If you are greedy and try to make him maintain it for longer, he will probably try to lie down.*

▶ **Step 3:** Start to hold the treat on the floor for a little longer; it may help if you hold the food under your hand so your palm is flat to the floor.

▶ **Step 4:** When dog performs a bow as you take your hand to the floor, you can introduce the verbal cue, "bend".

▶ **Step 5:** Now it's a case of repeating the move and increasing duration, but you still need to be there with the left hand so the dog doesn't collapse.

▶ **Step 6:** The next stage is to remove the food so that the dog starts to perform the trick on command. To do this, crouch down beside the dog and – when he is not looking – place a treat behind you. Just as before, take your right hand down to the floor, which is the signal for the dog to bow. As soon as he is in the correct position, quickly get the treat from behind your back and reward him while he maintains the bow. In this way, he will get used to the fact that the lure hand doesn't always have a treat in it but one will arrive, like magic, as soon as he performs a bow.

Gradually work on phasing out the food lure, and increasing duration.

Now withdraw your left, supporting hand.

▶ **Step 7:** As the dog becomes more accustomed to performing the move on command, you can progress to standing up beside him.

TOP TIP — *To prevent the dog getting stuck on you, try throwing the treat on to the floor in front of him, rather than rewarding from the hand. You can progress this so that you are able to point to the floor to signal the bow.*

Body Awareness

▶ **Step 8:** You can advance this trick by asking the dog to perform a bow from a distance. You can do this by either telling him to stand and wait, or you can place him behind a barrier. Make sure you always return to the dog to reward him, as this will prevent him coming forward. You can also build on the starter trick, *paws on a box* (see page 27) by asking the dog to bend while he has his front feet on the box.

Progression

Stand further away from the dog so he learns to perform the trick at a distance.

FEET IN A BOX

The trick

This trick, which involves the dog placing all four feet in a box, teaches the dog about using his back end. Many dogs will walk into the box with their front legs but cannot tuck their legs underneath them to get all four feet in at the same time. You may need several boxes, starting with a larger box and gradually moving down in size to a smaller box. The ideal box should be of sufficient size to allow the dog to stand in it comfortably. The sides should not be too high as the dog needs to step over it so, for a dog of Collie size, the sides should be around 20cm (8in) in height. The area of the box will depend on the size of the dog, but a rectangular box is ideal to start with as the dog can walk into it from one of the short ends and should at least get two paws, or more, in the box as he walks through.

To climb into a box (or any other container) and accommodate all four feet.

▶ **Step 1:** Position the box with one of the short ends facing the dog and, with a treat in your right hand, encourage him to walk through it. At this stage I suggest you kneel down and hold the box with your left hand, to keep it stable. If the dog has a negative experience with the box moving, he might take a long time to get over it. Some dogs are very cautious about placing their feet on a new surface, so you may need to spend time rewarding the dog for just putting one paw in the box. Don't be a greedy trainer and demand the dog puts all four paws in before he gets a reward.

▶ **Step 2:** At this stage it's all about building confidence so, initially, you will lure the dog into the box. You should find that he starts to anticipate the reward being given when he is in the box, so he will start getting in without your help. At this stage you can give the verbal command, "in", when the dog has got all four feet in the box – but make sure you don't give the cue too early.

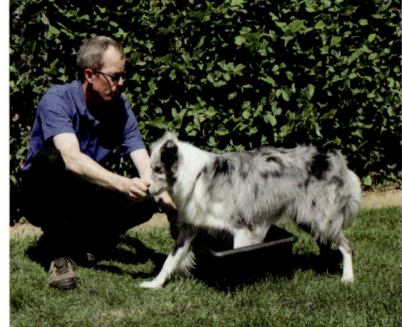

Initially reward for getting any feet in the box, and then wait until all four feet are in before rewarding.

▶ **Step 3:** When the dog has mastered the trick in a relatively big box, it's time to downsize. When you start using a smaller box, you may need to go back a stage or two and help the dog, as he might have become context orientated to placing his feet in the first box. Remember, the box is smaller, which means it is harder for the dog to accommodate all four feet. You may, therefore, need to go back to rewarding when he has two or three feet in the box.

▶ **Step 4:** At this stage the dog should be able to get in a box, even if it is still quite large. However, you have been kneeling down to encourage him, so the next step is to stand up and ask him to go "in", and to gradually fade your hand signals. To do this, make sure you signal with one hand but reward with the other.

Now stand up and ask the dog to go "in" the box. Gradually phase out the food and the hand signals.

Body Awareness   55

▶ **Step 5:** You can gradually decrease the size of the box, although how small you go will depend on your dog's size. As he becomes more confident, you can add distance by moving away from the box and asking the dog to go and get in it.

Progression

When the dog responds solely to a verbal cue, you can stand further back and ask him to go "in' the box from a distance.

SIDE PASS

The trick

Teaching the dog to walk to the side, like a crab, is another great way to develop coordination. This is one of the harder tricks, as the dog has to co-ordinate all four legs, and his body, at the same time.

If you have taught your dog *pirouette* on a box (see page 48) you will have sown the seed of moving to the side with his back legs. A word of warning: do not teach this move and a *walk back* (see page 31) at the same time. Both start with the dog in front of you, so he is likely to get confused.

▶ **Step 1:** Position the dog so he is standing in front of you. You will need a treat in your right hand, and you will be moving to *your* left. Start by luring the dog, with your right hand, so that he turns his head towards his

The dog walks in a sideways direction.

left elbow. As the dog turns his head, his back end should move to your left. As this is happening, turn to your left in a circle. Imagine doing *pirouette on a box*, but without the box. Try to keep both feet on the spot so you can turn in a tight circle. If you drift sideways, moving around the dog, you will not encourage him to move his back end.

The start position.

Using the treat, lure the dog so he is turning his head to his left elbow.

As the dog turns his head, turn in a tight circle to your left.

▶ **Step 2:** The dog should now be moving around sideways as you turn his head and pivot on the spot. At this stage you can reward the dog with his head facing you rather than rewarding the turned head. You might need to mix between turning his head to get him started, then turning it back in order to keep him straight. Introduce the "side" command as the dog is moving his body to the side.

▶ **Step 3:** Until now the dog has been performing this trick while you pivot around to your left in an anti-clockwise circle. In order for the dog to perform it moving in a straight line to your left, rather than in a circle, you need to get him to side pass part of a circle and then walk to the side for a couple of paces to your left. Gradually reduce the pivot as the dog becomes more proficient at performing a straight-line side pass.

▶ **Step 4:** At this stage you have probably held the food very near to the dog's nose in order to keep him straight. To start phasing this out, place the food in a fist so the dog cannot nibble it and will, therefore, think a little more. Over time, move your hands closer to your body.

Hold the treat in a fist and gradually withdraw your hands.

Body Awareness

> **TOP TIP** *When you working on moving your hands further from the dog, go back to doing the side pass circle so that he has the physical cue of your body turning.*

At this stage, you may find the dog is not as precise with his sideways movement, so make sure you turn his head to your right when giving a reward. This encourages him to adjust his weight and, thus, his deportment, enabling him to perform a perfect side pass.

▶ **Step 5:** Now that the side pass is on cue, and you don't need your hands to signal the move, you can experiment with making it harder. One way of doing this is ask the dog to perform it while at a distance. To teach the side pass at a distance, place the dog behind a barrier, which is about the height of the dog and around 2-3 metres (6-9ft) in length. Gradually move away from the barrier and ask the dog to perform the side pass when he is behind it. Remember to go back to him, every time, to reward him, as this will ensure that he doesn't come towards you.

Once you have added distance to the move when the dog is facing you, a further option is teach the dog to side pass while facing your back.

SIT ON A BLOCK

The trick

The dog sits on a raised platform.

This is another good move to make your dog aware of his back legs. If you have already taught *paws on a box* (see page 27), you will need to be careful you don't ruin it by starting work on this trick at the same time. In the early stages of training, a good way of making a distinction is to use a different object for each trick. When you are working on *paws on a box*, the box can be a lot smaller than the block you require when you are asking the dog to sit on it.

On a practical note, make sure the block has a non-slip surface, such as rubber or carpet that is stuck to the top. The block can be anywhere between 5-20cm

(2-8in) in height. Just as with *feet in a box* (see page 53), you may need to start with a bigger block and gradually work down in size if the dog is struggling to get all four paws on it. You also need to ensure the block is sufficiently stable so that the dog is not in danger of falling off it. A bad experience, at this stage, could take many weeks to overcome.

▶ **Step 1:** First of all encourage the dog towards the block and reward him for any interaction with it.

> **TOP TIP** *To encourage the dog to interact with the block, and particularly when you are luring him to place any of his feet on it (step 2), position the block between yourself and a wall to create a channel to it.*

▶ **Step 2:** With the block in front of you and the dog on your left, kneel down and use your right hand, holding food, to lure the dog across the block. If required, use your left hand to keep it still. Try to keep the dog's head level, rather than looking upwards, as you lure him across the block. Be ready to mark with your clicker, or clicker word, when you get two, or more, of his feet touching it. Don't be greedy and wait for all four feet. In order to keep his focus and interest, reward random efforts, so sometimes for three feet, or two. If you see that the dog is consistently not using a foot, move the reward left or right in front of him as he goes across the block. This should change his deportment so he should start use the leg.

Encourage the dog to place his front paws on the block.

▶ **Step 3:** Start to introduce the "on" command when the dog has all four paws on the block. As he becomes more confident, you can progress from kneeling by the block to standing up.

▶ **Step 4:** The dog should now almost instantly go to the block and stand on it, so you can now reward a sit or any position your dog can hold.

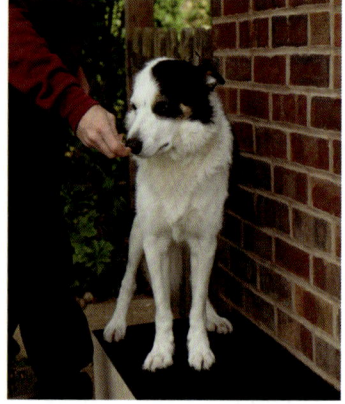

Wait until he consistently places four feet on the block before introducing your verbal cue.

Body Awareness

You can now move the block to a more open location and ask him to get on it.

Work on the sit, or any other static position.

▶ **Step 5:** In order to progress this trick, start to stand further away. If you have been using a hand signal to send the dog to the block, start to decrease the use of this.

Progression

To advance the move, add distance and fade out hand signals.

REVERSE

The trick

Reversing from a distance between your legs

This trick involves the dog reversing through your legs from a distance and is brilliant for teaching back end awareness

Firstly, you may need to brush up on your dog's sit and wait skills as, when he starts to anticipate the move, he will reverse before he is asked. Although we don't want this, it can be seen as a sign that the dog is growing in confidence, which means you can position him further away from you.

▶ **Step 1:** Stand with your feet together, and with the dog sitting on your left hand-side. Tell him to "wait" and move your left foot across his back end. If he stays in a sit, step back, and reward him for staying in position. Repeat but, this time, hold a food treat, discreetly, in your left hand. Place your right hand in front of the dog to prevent him from coming forwards. If you have a larger dog, encourage him to stand as this will make it easier for him to reverse in the early stages. Now place your left hand behind your left leg and touch the dog on his left side. This should encourage him to investigate and, thus, reverse backwards through your legs where you will reward him.

Step across the dog's back end, while telling him to wait.

Position your right hand to prevent him coming forward.

The touch of your left hand should encourage him to step back through your legs.

▶ **Step 2:** Sometimes, after only a few goes, the dog will understand that he needs to reverse, as he knows this is where the food will be. As he is reversing, introduce the "verse" command, but make sure you do this while he is performing the move – not before he starts it. At this stage you may need to reward the dog for sitting still more times than you reward him for performing a reverse, as he will be starting to anticipate the move.

▶ **Step 3:** Now that the dog has the behaviour on cue, you can stand a short distance from the back end of the dog in order to extend the reverse distance. If you go too far, too soon, you will find that the dog starts to reverse but will then stop to look round at you. Therefore, you need to work out how far to stand behind the dog. When extending the distance, mix up longer and shorter distances to maintain the dog's enthusiasm and to build his confidence.

Gradually stand further from the dog's back end. Remember to give your verbal cue as the dog is reversing.

▶ **Step 4:** Increase the distance that you can stand behind the dog until you are 2-3m (6-9 ft) from his back end, and he can reverse unaided.

TOP TIP

When you are working on extending the distances of the reverse, it helps it you give the dog some guidelines, such as a wall and a few chairs to form a channel. Place the chairs side by side, with the backs of the chairs facing the wall. Start by making the channel a little wider than your dog – if it is too narrow he may feel intimidated.

▶ **Step 5:** Progress the trick by moving back while the dog reverses, so you are mirroring what he is doing. You might also ask him to stop in a sit, or *take a bow* (see page 51), when he has reversed part of the way. To do this, the additional move – the sit or the bow – needs to be on a reliable verbal cue as the dog will have his back to you and, therefore, cannot rely on hand signals.

Progression

Mirror what the dog is doing back by walking backwards as he reverses.

RAISE A BACK LEG

The trick

Getting the dog to give you one of his front paws is relatively easy, but you may find it takes you a while to get the dog to think about his back legs. This demands both balance and back end awareness.

Lifting a back leg, on cue.

▶ **Step 1:** Location is important for this trick. Kneel on the floor, with the dog parallel to you, facing your left hand. You need a wall on the other side of the dog so he has something to lean against when he is trying to balance. As the dog is facing your left hand, which has a treat in it, you will be working on the back leg nearest to you, i.e. the dog's left hind.

▶ **Step 2:** Holding a treat to your dog's nose with your left hand, place your right hand under the left hind paw as if scooping it up. The dog may lift his leg or he may place his paw on to your hand. Mark either of these behaviours with a click, or your clicker word – but don't insist he holds his paw on your hand – and reward from your left hand. In the early stages of training, the dog may raise his paw for no more than a millisecond, but this should be rewarded. Building duration on this move comes much later.

Keep the dog's focus by holding a treat in your left hand and use your right hand to scoop up his left hind paw.

Reward for placing the paw on your hand, or for a momentary lift of the leg.

▶ **Step 3:** The dog should be used to you scooping up his paw so that it is resting on your hand. At this stage, you can introduce your verbal cue – I use "tootsie". The dog should then start to pick up his paw, as he anticipates your hand coming in, and understands he must place it on your hand. Bear in mind, it may take a fair number of training sessions, spread over several days, to get to this stage.

Body Awareness   63

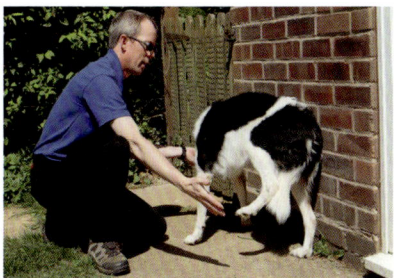

Over time, the dog will start to lift his paw as he anticipates your hand coming in to scoop it up.

Hold your hand a little higher to encourage a higher leg left.

▶ **Step 4:** You will have been holding your hand fairly close to the floor to encourage the dog to rest his paw on it. You now need to repeat step 3, but hold your hand a little higher. Each dog will have his own preferences as to how high to raise the paw, and some dogs extend the leg backwards rather than upwards. Your job is to observe the dog closely and focus on what he finds most comfortable.

▶ **Step 5:** This stage is all about extending the duration of the leg in the air rather than when it is on the hand. To start with, ask the dog to raise his paw and, when it hits your hand, briefly remove it from the paw and then return it. The dog should anticipate the hand coming back in and will, therefore, not put it back down on the floor. Mark and reward any extension of the time the dog is holding his leg in suspension. However, you must always remember to reward randomly – both shorter and longer duration – so that you are not continually asking for longer and longer periods.

▶ **Step 6:** Up until now you will have been kneeling beside the dog, so now you need to stand up, but still give the dog a prompt with your right hand touching his left hind, if necessary. You also need to phase out the food, which you have been holding close to the dog's mouth. In order to do this, use your verbal cue, "tootsie" to ask for the leg lift, then take the food away for a second and return it to feed the dog. You may need to help by using your right hand to remind him to keep his paw in the air, even though the food is not near his nose. This will, gradually, accustom him to performing the move without relying on the food being close to his nose.

▶ **Step 7:** In order to start to proof the trick, work on asking for the leg lift while the dog is in different places.

To complete the trick, stand up when you ask for it. You can then try taking it to different locations.

However, you will probably find that he needs some help to get started, as he will be conditioned to performing the trick in the place where you first trained it.

▶ **Step 8:** Now you have trained the left hind leg lift, you are ready to repeat the whole process, this time working on the right hind.

▶ **Step 9:** You can advance this trick by getting the dog to 'cock his leg' against an object. To do this, get a chair and condition the dog to standing near it while you cue the paw lift. As the dog gets more used to performing the trick beside the chair, he will anticipate it. At this stage you can work on sending the dog to the chair to perform the move.

Progression

This trick looks more impressive when you add distance, and match what the dog is doing by raising your leg on the same side.

WAVE

The trick

This trick is one of the more challenging, as it requires the dog to lift one front and one back leg, on the same side, while leaning against your leg. This demands a fine degree of balance, which cannot be achieved overnight. You will need to spend many weeks building a good foundation for this trick.

In the first few weeks of training, you can work on the bottom step of a flight of stairs, as this will give the dog confidence in placing two legs, from the same side, on a flat raised

The dog raises front and back legs on the same side.

surface. You can then progress to using a board, with a non-slip surface. It should be just a little longer than the dog, and 15cm (6in) higher than the height of the dog, measuring from the top of his shoulders.

▶ **Step 1:** Lean the board against a wall so that it is angled. At all times make sure the board will not slip down; check this by placing your foot on the board near the top. For this trick you will be working to get the dog's left front and back paws on to the board. To start, position the dog on your left side while you face the board. Encourage the dog to place any paw on the board by luring him across the board with your right hand. If he is reluctant to put a foot on the board, take it from the wall and prop it up with something lower until the dog is happy going on and off it.

In the early days, don't insist on both paws on the board at once.

▶ **Step 2:** Prop the board against the wall and place your left foot at the bottom of it. With a treat in your right hand, encourage the dog in a U shape, around your left leg, from your left side. Manipulate the food over the next few training sessions so that you reward for, perhaps, his left front paw on the board, or maybe his back legs on the board. Bear in mind, you may not get both left front and hind paws on at the same time in the first few sessions.

TOP TIPS   *To get the first stage:*

- Move your foot lower if you are getting too many paws on the board.

- Bend the dog around your leg as if you are turning the dog's head towards the inside of your left leg. This should encourage him to put his left front, or back, paw on the board.

- If you are getting the back leg on but not the front paw, don't turn the dog's head towards you. Try to keep his head straighter.

Turn the dog's head away from you to encourage him to push against your leg.

▶ **Step 3:** At this stage, the dog should be standing across you with his front and back left paws against the board. Now that he is happy to do this with the food close to his nose, you can encourage him to lean against your left leg so that he can perform the trick without the board. It is very important to keep your leg as straight as possible to give the dog something secure to lean against. There is a tendency for handlers to lean away from the dog, which – from the dog's perspective – feels less secure and may make him reluctant to perform the move.

Hold the board with your left hand as if it was propped against a wall.

With your foot still low down on the board, ask the dog to put both paws on the board, and then reward him with his head turned away from you so that he pushes against your leg. At this stage you want the dog to get used to leaning against the leg – but not too much. If he has a tendency to lean too heavily, make sure you reward him with a straighter head, i.e. facing off to your right. You should still have the reward, in your right hand, to lure the dog, but place it in your fist so he cannot get at it straightaway. If the treat is secured in your fist, you can let him have a few attempts without grabbing the food. But as soon as he has got it right – if only for a second – open your hand and feed him.

▶ **Step 4:** This is probably the most difficult stage and the one that takes the longest. You now need to get the dog to release his feet from the board so that he is just leaning against your leg. To do this, hold the board with your left hand, as if it was propped against the wall. Use your right hand, as before, to get the dog into position. Then, when he is standing with both feet on the board, start to wobble it very slightly. This will make him remove one of his feet – just for a second – and then to place it back on the board. You need to be super alert and mark the moment his foot is in the air. This stage is all about developing the dog's balance, so you will need to take your time, and reward frequently.

Gradually move the board further away and reward the instant the dog raises one – and then both legs – without needing to use the board.

Body Awareness 67

> **TOP TIP** *When you are working on improving balance, you can try positioning the dog near the board, but hold it just that little bit too far from him when he is standing parallel to you. If the dog has been conditioned correctly to get his paws on the board, you will probably find he will attempt to do this, and may raise one of his feet. Remember to reward this as the dog is making a progression from feet on the board to feet in the air.*

▶ **Step 5:** By now, the dog should be leaning against you and raising both legs – for just a second – with the board nearby. It's a good idea to keep the board near to the dog while you are building duration so that you can mark with your clicker, or clicker word, when his feet are off the board but then he can rest his paws on the board while receiving his treat. In this way, the dog is being rewarded with his legs raised – not when they are back in the floor. At this stage you can introduce your verbal cue, "wave" as the trick is near to being finished.

▶ **Step 6:** Now the dog has the move on command, you can start to stand up straighter and extend the time period for the holding the position.

> **TOP TIP** *While working on this trick, you may have got into a habit of holding your hands in a certain way to lure the dog into position. The best plan is to video yourself when performing the trick, as this can help you to fine-tune the move – for example, removing a hand, or a hesitation.*

▶ **Step 7:** Up to now you will have remained static while working on this trick. One of the harder things to do is walk forward with the dog, then ask for the wave position. First of all walk forward, very slowly, with the dog on the left. When you ask him to wave, hold the flat of your left hand to make a mini board along his left side, which should help him into position without a delay. Gradually increase your speed before stopping and asking for the wave.

Chapter 6: Core Strength, Stretching and Flexibilty

A sports dog is an athlete and, as such, his body must be primed for the work he has to do. Core strength, stretching and flexibility can all be developed with a directed fitness programme, but this is hard work, and can be tedious for both you, and your dog.

Trick training is a way of making your dog a willing participant in his fitness regime and, better still, he will be exercising his mind as well as his body.

The tricks outlined in this chapter will help to develop:

Core strength: This relates to the centre of your dog's body; it is a stabilising force, which allows him to move in any direction with ease. Core strength is, therefore, of paramount importance to all sports dogs, allowing them to perform the required exercises effectively and with minimal risk of injury

Stretching: This is a form of exercise that targets specific muscles in the dog's body in order to improve their elasticity and to increase muscle tone. This allows the dog to perform to the best of his ability and, again, reduces the risk of injury.

Flexibility: This is more specifically related to the dog's joints and how freely they move. It ties in with the mobility of the muscles, which facilitate movement around the joints. When the dog is competing in any discipline his joints needs to be super supple so that they can react to commands at speed.

To perform these tricks, the dog needs to find his balance as well as being able to bend and flex his body. Tricks that require balance need to be built up gradually so, in the initial stages of training, the dog should only be expected to hold position for just a second or two. Resist the temptation to ask for too much, too soon, as he may not have the strength to hold the position. The same applies to moves which require the dog to stretch, or flex, a specific part of his body. When you are training the dog to lower or raise his head, for example, you will need to progress by degrees, allowing the muscles to develop the required strength and flexibility to perform the move.

STICK 'EM UP

The trick

This is a fun trick in which the dog turns away from you and places his feet on the wall behind him. The benefit of this move is it gets the dog to stretch upwards when his feet are on the wall.

To start this move, you need to encourage your dog to place his feet on a variety of surfaces. This has the added bonus of developing his proprioceptive skills – his body awareness and motor skills – which are needed for contact equipment in agility and prop work in freestyle and heelwork to music.

So when you are out on a walk with your dog, reward him for placing his feet on random objects, such as a park bench, a log, or a rubbish bin. This will help to build his confidence in touching different objects, so when you ask him to place his feet on the wall for this trick, he will be happy to do so.

The dog turns his back on you and places his front paws on a wall.

▶ **Step 1:** To start this trick, encourage the dog to place his paws on a wall. When you do this, make sure you don't hold the food too high otherwise he will jump upwards, which will be the start of a bad habit. Hold a treat by the dog's nose and, imagining the dog is being pulled upwards by a thread of cotton, lure him on to the wall so his paws are against it. To prepare the dog for later, start to randomise the time you require the dog to stay in position before rewarding him.

Lure the dog so he places his front paws on a wall.

▶ **Step 2:** To teach the next element, position yourself facing the wall, with the dog facing you. Turn the dog anti-clockwise with your right hand so that he is facing the wall, and reward with a treat from your right hand. Repeat the turn several times. When the dog is facing the wall, encourage him to turn back the way he went into the move. This will stop him getting used to turning all the way around, as he did for *Twist* (see page 19).

Facing the wall, use your right hand to turn the dog anti-clockwise so that he is also facing the wall.

▶ **Step 3:** Having mastered the first two steps, you can now join them together, encouraging the dog to place his feet up on the wall when he has turned away from you.

▶ **Step 4:** When the dog understands what is required, introduce the "stick 'em up" command. Give the verbal cue when the dog is first on the wall, then start dropping it in earlier before he gets there.

▶ **Step 5:** Now it's time to remove the food lure. Take the dog around with your right hand but, when he is up on the wall, use your left hand to reward him.

▶ **Step 6:** Decrease the right hand signal until the dog will turn and place his feet on the wall just on the vocal command. Now you need to add duration so he doesn't come down off the wall in the first few seconds. To do this, hold your right hand above the dog to encourage him to stay in position, and reward with several small treats so that he is not tempted to move.

Now combine both elements so he turns away from you and places his paws on the wall. Fade the food lure, and use your right hand to signal and your left hand to reward.

When the dog is responding to a verbal cue – with no hand signals – you can work on duration.

SIT PRETTY

The trick

The beg, or sit pretty, is one of the best tricks for developing core strength. It is important to wait until the dog is fully grown before starting this move – it is definitely not something you would do with a puppy. If you have a larger dog it might be better to teach him a supported beg, in which his front feet are allowed to touch you, or an object, when he is in the beg in order to provide better stability.

One of the common problems when teaching this move is that the handler raises the dog's head too high over his back. This makes the dog hop backwards out of the sit position, or stand up on his hind legs. So when you are rewarding the dog, try to keep his head in a level position.

The dog goes into a 'beg' position.

▶ **Step 1:** Start with the dog in the sit position, on your left side. The food should be in the palm of your right hand, held down by your thumb. Place the food on the dog's nose and raise it up very slightly; you want the dog to reach forward over the edge of your hand for the food. At this point, you should be rewarding when the front feet come off the ground for a millisecond. A common problem among handlers is asking for duration on this move, too soon.

If the dog lifts his front paws just a fraction from the ground, be ready to reward.

▶ **Step 2:** You will need to constantly adjust the height, and placement, of your hand in order to get the dog to sit and raise his paws, so make sure you only do a few repetitions before giving the dog a break. It takes a while for the dog to develop the balance required for this move.

TOP TIP *If your dog is struggling, you can ask him to give a paw to your hand before encouraging him to beg. This gives him some stability so he should find it easier to raise the other leg.*
A word of warning: *If you continue to allow the dog to rest his paw on your hand, this will become part of the move. If this happens, go back to step one and reward the dog for raising his front feet off the ground, just a short distance.*

▶ **Step 3:** When the dog is coming up into the beg position for a second or two, you can introduce a verbal cue, "both" or "pretty". To increase duration, hold the food in your fist and then open and feed when he has maintained position for the required length of time. However, even at this stage, you need to be careful and not ask the dog to maintain position for too long.

To increase duration, hold the treat in your fist, pause when the dog is in position, and then open it to reward.

▶ **Step 4:** The dog should now be sitting pretty for a good few seconds so it's time to fade the lure hand. Over time, stand up and hold your hand a little further from his head. Gradually, hold your signal hand closer to your chest before you ask the dog to beg. Your aim is to ask for the trick, on cue, with your hands behind your back.

> **TOP TIP** When you are phasing out the hand signal, use your hand to help the dog into the beg position, but then bring the other hand in to reward him. This way, the dog starts to learn that it doesn't need the food on his nose to get into position.

Fade the lure and, gradually, reduce your hand signal.

▶ **Step 5:** When the dog is proficient at performing *sit pretty*, on cue, you can enhance the move with a number of variations. For example, ask for a *sit pretty* from a distance, or at the end of *walk back* (see page 31). When the dog is really confident and has developed good core strength and balance, you can ask for a *sit pretty* when he is in a box, as an extension of *feet in a box* (see page 53).

Progression

Combine two tricks and ask for *sit pretty* in a box.

Core Strength, Stretching and Flexibilty

SAY YOUR PRAYERS

The trick

This is a lovely trick, which conveys that the dog is 'ashamed' or 'naughty' as he places his head between his front legs. It really helps the dog to develop internal core stability as well as stretching the back muscles.

This trick is easier to teach if the dog already knows *paws on a box* (see page 27) as he needs to raise his front feet off the ground. If you haven't already taught this trick, encourage the dog to place his front paws on your leg, or on your arm, which will also allow him to place his head between his front legs.

The dog places his front feet on a raised surface and lowers his head between them.

▶ **Step 1:** Encourage the dog to stand with his front feet on a chair; he should be positioned on your left hand-side. Make sure you have a treat in both hands.

▶ **Step 2:** With the dog's front feet on the chair, kneel beside him and place your right hand on his nose to distract him. Now stretch your left arm through his front legs as far as you can reach. Remove your right hand from the dog's nose and encourage him to take a treat from your left hand by bobbing his head downwards. As soon as the

Lure the dog so he places his front feet on a raised surface – in this case, a chair.

dog has eaten the reward from your left hand, move your right hand, holding the treat, back on his nose to encourage him to stand up. This last part is important, as if the dog follows your left hand as you withdraw it, he will slip off the chair. Remember, you want the dog's front feet to remain on the chair all the time. If one paw moves off – it's usually the right paw, the one closest to you – it is because your left arm is not low enough as you reach through his front legs. You can remedy this by stretching through the dog's front legs but, rather than letting him eat the treat from your hand, place it on the chair. This helps the dog to maintain position, as he is not following your left hand as you take it away.

Stretch your left arm through his front legs, so he has to lower his head to take a treat from your left hand.

Now use the treat in your right hand to raise his head.

▶ **Step 3:** For the first few attempts, don't expect the dog to lower his head very far between his front legs. As with any trick, don't ask for too much, too soon. Over the next few sessions, work on giving multiple treats while the dog's head is lowered, but make sure he is allowed to stand every time he has done the trick. He needs to get used to stretching his neck muscles as he does this trick, so allow him to become more flexible before taking his head lower.

▶ **Step 4:** As the dog gets used to the move, you can encourage him to place his head lower between his front legs by not reaching as far through his front legs with your left hand. You can now introduce the verbal cue, "pray", as he lowers his head between his front legs.

The dog will hold his lead lower if you don't stretch so far through his front legs.

Core Strength, Stretching and Flexibilty

▶ **Step 5:** At this stage the dog should have a good idea of what is expected, so you are ready to phase out your left hand, which is encouraging him to drop his head.

First, place your left hand in position – but lower than normal – before asking the dog to "pray". It helps if you hold the treat in your fist so he cannot instantly grab it. You will still need to distract him with a treat in your right hand on his nose, before and after the move, to prevent him slipping off the chair. As you give your verbal cue, the dog will, hopefully, go into the position, allowing you to raise your left hand to reward him.

Over time, do not stretch your arm so far underneath the dog's body and, gradually, lower your left hand still further. Bear in mind you are changing the look of the trick, so you need to reward for shorter periods when he holds position. If the dog is trying hard to perform the move, be ready to reward him, even if it's not perfect.

▶ **Step 6:** The last stage is to teach the dog to perform it without the left lure hand. To do this, feed the dog a treat when he is in position, as you have done before, but now momentarily withdraw the hand from sight, bringing it back quickly to feed him again. This accustoms the dog to holding the position without relying on the left hand. As he gains confidence, he should start to duck his head, when asked, without needing the left hand to be visible.

▶ **Step 7:** Now the dog has learnt the trick, you can ask for it when you are standing, and when he is positioned at a distance. You can also ask him to "pray" while resting his front paws on your arm. If you want to really push the move you can join up *sit pretty* (see page 71) and ask the dog to "pray" while his front paws are resting on an object, such as a box or chair.

The final stage is to stand up and to phase out the left hand lure.

POPPING FROM DOWN TO BOW

The trick

In Chapter Three, featuring tricks for body awareness, I outlined how to teach your dog to *take a bow* (see page 51) from the stand. This involves the dog using his front end to go down to the floor while keeping its back end raised. Now the aim is to teach the dog to go from the down position and 'pop' into the bow. This is a different movement for the dog, as he has to keep his front end on the floor and raise his back end.

Starting from a down and going into a bow.

This trick is good for stretching the dog's rear muscles – a move you will often see when a dog gets up after resting and stretches in a bow position.

▶ **Step 1:** Kneel on the floor with the dog parallel to you in a down position. You need a reward in your right hand.

▶ **Step 2:** Firstly, move your right hand (holding a treat) towards the dog's chest. Keep your hand very close to the floor with the palm facing upwards. Meanwhile, use your left hand to tickle the dog, just inside his right back leg. The should encourage him to kick up his back end, while your right hand is keeping his front end down on the floor.

With the dog in a down, hold a treat in your right hand and use your left hand to tickle just inside his right back leg.

The contact from your left hand will encourage the dog to raise his hindquarters while the treat in your right hand will ensure his forequarters stay on the ground.

If this doesn't work, maybe due to the dog's size, there is another option. Try moving your right hand, with the palm facing downwards, forwards along the floor so that it is travelling, very slowly, away from the dog. This is your lure hand, holding a treat, so the dog should follow it.

Meanwhile, insert your left hand in front of the dog's right back leg to keep him in the bow. You will need to be careful about bringing the dog forward as he may well stand up. To prevent this, make sure you move your right hand across the floor, keeping it close to the dog's nose. You want the dog to move forwards very slightly – just enough to raise his back end.

▶ **Step 3:** When the dog becomes proficient at kicking up his back legs, introduce the verbal cue, "pop", as he raises his back end. You are now ready to, gradually, phase out your right hand, which you have been using to lure the dog forwards. When he goes into a bow, feed him several small rewards from the right so that he learns to hold the position until told otherwise.

▶ **Step 4:** Now work on standing up while the dog performs the move, rather than kneeling on the floor. Initially you may need to bend over, so that your hands are more at floor level, as the dog will associate this positioning with the move.

Gradually withdraw your left hand so the dog goes into position without the physical prompt.

At this stage you want the dog to perform the trick without food in the right hand. So use the right hand to signal, and the left hand to reward the dog in the bow position. Mix between releasing the dog from the bow, and letting him come forward and lying down so that he can perform the trick again.

▶ **Step 5:** You can progress this move by teaching the dog to pop into position when he sees you bend forward, thus mirroring your movement. To do this, give the verbal cue, "pop", and – at the same time – perform the action. Over time you will find the dog will no longer need the vocal command but will respond to your visual cue. This is a fun trick to perform – and it's great for improving your dog's flexibility.

Progression

Mirror the dog's move by bending over as he goes into a bow.

ROLL-OVER

The trick

Starting from a down position, the dog executes a complete roll-over.

The roll-over requires both strength and coordination. If you are lucky this may be a move that your dog performs naturally. However, some dogs find the position – being on their back – makes them feel insecure. Therefore you need to give lots of positive reinforcement when teaching this move. If your dog continues to show reluctance, it may be best to give it up and work on a trick that he finds more enjoyable.

Before you start teaching the roll-over, you must first teach your dog to go into the down position correctly, as some dogs have a tendency to throw themselves to the floor when in the stand. Remind your dog of his "down", and keep rewarding him, to give value to the position. Remember, you want the dog to be in a sphinx position, with his back legs tucked underneath his body. As an additional safety measure, remember to leave a gap between the dog going into the down and asking for the roll-over – perhaps counting to five – to ensure he is 100 per cent secure in the down before he performs the trick.

Core Strength, Stretching and Flexibilty 79

▶ **Step 1:** Ask the dog to go into the down position and kneel in front of him. With a treat in your right hand, encourage him to turn his head to *his* left side. This will help him to go into a relaxed down with his right front leg underneath his body, and both back legs out to the side. If you see the dog tensing his body, you may need to stay at this stage for a while, rewarding and reinforcing his behaviour. He needs to be comfortable, lying in a relaxed down position, before you continue.

The start position.

Turn the dog's head to his left side which will encourage him to go into a relaxed down.

▶ **Step 2:** When the dog is in the relaxed down position, use the treat in your right hand to turn his head, as before, in an anti-clockwise direction, as if to go over his back. Some dogs might worry, at this stage, as they feel unstable. It is, therefore, important to take it very slowly, giving lots of rewards and praise. You want the dog to be reaching around for the treat and, in so doing, he will almost start the roll-over.

▶ **Step 3:** When the dog is confident in the previous step, lure his head further over his body, which will result in him 'accidentally' starting to roll. Make sure you have a high value, jackpot reward, as this will encourage him to make the effort to roll right over. When the dog is following the food, and performing the roll-over, you can introduce your verbal cue for the trick – "roll".

Very gradually, keep turning the dog's head anti-clockwise until...

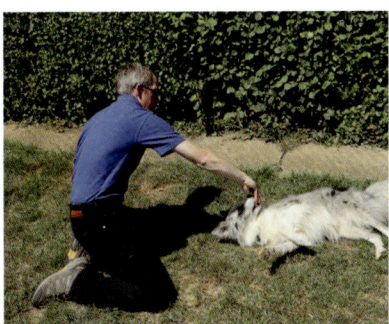
...he 'accidentally' starts to roll over.

▶ **Step 4:** Still using the food as a lure, let the dog follow the treat over his body but, this time, bring his head back so it is facing straight towards you. This should help him to go back to the down, which will be useful when you want to perform multiple roll-overs, one after another, as he is returning to the correct, sphinx position.

Now work on luring the dog's head over his body for the roll-over, but then bring his head back so that it is facing you, which will allow him to return to the down position.

TOP TIP *It may be that the dog goes into a relaxed down, rather than adopting the correct sphinx position, when you are turning his head to face you. If this happens, encourage him to reach forward to get the treat, as this will encourage him to position his back legs underneath his body.*

▶ **Step 5:** Now it's time to ask the dog to perform the move without the food on his nose. To do this, use your right hand to help him, and give the verbal cue. When he has completed the roll-over, reward with a treat from your left hand. As the dog becomes proficient, try standing up, first keeping your hand low then, gradually, standing up straighter and phasing out your right hand.

At this stage, be careful, as some dogs have a tendency to leap up after the roll to get the reward quicker. Therefore you need to ensure you always reward when the dog is in the correct, down position. This might mean you need to give your "down" cue after the roll, or just be quick delivering the treat when he is in the down.

Core Strength, Stretching and Flexibilty

▶ **Step 6:** The dog should now be able to perform this trick, on cue, without hand signals. At this stage you are ready to stand further away from the dog before asking him to "roll". When he is confident rolling to his right, you can repeat all the steps and teach him to roll-over to the left. This will need a different verbal cue – I use "other".

TOP TIP *When you are teaching the dog to roll in a new direction, don't practise doing both moves in succession – a right roll-over followed by a left roll-over, for example – as the dog will start second guessing and not complete the first roll before he rolls back over.*

Chapter 7

Focus and Thinking

So far, I have focused on teaching tricks in which the dog has to use his body. Now it's time to get him to use his brain! Sports and performance dogs need to concentrate, regardless of distractions, and they also need to process instructions when they are under pressure. The tricks outlined in this chapter will help your dog to develop his powers of concentration and he will become a more flexible thinker as he applies his mind to different tasks. Best of all, the tricks are rewarding and fun to perform, and will provide a productive, yet light-hearted, interlude in your training programme.

Remember, mental fatigue is just as much a factor as physical fatigue so be careful not to over-practise these tricks in any one training session. The moves involved require a good deal of processing so it will take the dog some time to reach a full understanding.

When training these tricks, give the dog a chance to compute what you are asking of him, rather than instantly helping him. There are times when it is better not to say, or do, anything. If the dog has some thinking time, he may try again and then you can give him extra praise and multiple rewards.

All dogs are different. The thinkers will find these tricks relatively straightforward; those that are more like a bull in a china shop will find them more challenging. However, if you work at a pace that suits your own, individual dog, and provide plenty of positive reinforcement, he will develop both mental strength, and the ability to learn.

DISTANCE BACK UP

The trick

If you have taught your dog to *walk back* (see page 31) you will have already sown the seed for this trick. You are now building on this foundation and asking the dog to back up, over a distance, on his own. The *walk back* involves the handler moving towards the dog, and he may be able to cover a reasonable distance with this degree of signalling. Now he has to learn to back up without the assistance of the handler moving towards him, which may be a stumbling block in the early training of this trick. However overcoming this issue, by encouraging the dog to think for himself, will be beneficial in progressing your trick training, and in your chosen discipline.

An extended walk back, without assistance from the handler.

To teach a distance back up, you will require either a mat or a platform. If you are working with a mat, it needs to be of sufficient size to accommodate the dog's front feet, and it must be different in texture from the floor. If you are working with a platform, it must accommodate the dog when he is standing four-square, with approximately 5cm (2in) to spare, – and it should be raised 5-7cm (2-3in) from the floor. You can teach a distance walk back with either of these pieces of equipment. However, the raised platform gives a clearer signal to the dog, as he has to step back on to it, whereas a mat can be mistaken for floor. I will, therefore, refer to a platform in the step-by-step instructions.

▶ **Step 1:** Encourage the dog to walk on to the platform by using a food reward. Click, or use your clicker word, when he has all four feet on it, and reward. Repeat this until you can stand near to the platform and the dog positions himself on it without any help. The dog should have a strong draw to the platform because he has been rewarded for going on it, so he should almost anticipate what you want him to do.

When the dog has all four feet on the platform, reward him in position.

▶ **Step 2:** Make sure the dog is facing you when he is on the platform. Using a treat as a lure, encourage him to take his front feet off the platform. Then remove the treat from sight by putting your hands behind your back.

If learning has been established in step 1, the dog should step back with his front feet so he is back on the platform, where he can be rewarded. If he doesn't move back on to the platform, help him out by taking a step towards it, which will signal where he needs to be. You will need to work on this element of training – sometimes allowing two feet off the platform, and sometimes all four feet – so the dog learns that his job is to step back on to the platform.

Don't be in a hurry to increase the dog's distance from the platform; in the early stages, he needs to build his confidence over short distances. When the dog clearly understands what is required, introduce the verbal cue, "walk back," as the dog is stepping back on to the platform.

Use a treat to lure him so he moves forward with his front feet and steps off the platform.

Withdraw the treat – putting your hand behind your back. The dog should step back on to the platform as he knows he is rewarded in this position.

▶ **Step 3:** Gradually extend the dog's starting point so he is further from the platform but, for every longer distance you ask for, make sure you reward a shorter distance next time. You also need to be careful with reward placement at this stage. If you throw the food to the dog he may come forward, anticipating the verbal cue. Therefore, the best plan is to return to the dog, swivel into his left side so he is in the left hand heelwork position, and then reward.

Extend the starting point so the dog has to cover a greater distance to reach the platform.

▶ **Step 4:** You are now ready to phase out the platform. To do this, click, or use your clicker word, when the dog is halfway back to the platform, and then return to him to reward. Mix up rewarding the dog when he is on the platform, and when he is walking back to it. Over time, he will learn to to perform the trick without the platform acting as a cue.

Phase out the platform.

▶ **Step 5:** To advance this trick you could attach various moves on the end of the walk back such as *the twist* (see page 19) or *take a bow* (see page 51). You can also change your position in relation to the dog before asking for the move. So, for example, you could turn your back to the dog and then ask him to "walk back".

Progression

Turn your back on the dog and then ask him to walk back.

LOOK LEFT AND RIGHT

For this trick there is both a basic and an advanced version that you can teach your dog. A fair amount of mental processing is required for both, and there is an element of impulse control in the advanced option, which is particularly useful for high-drive dogs. In addition, you can work on this trick if your dog has limited mobility – if he is recovering from injury, for example and you want to keep him occupied. Initially, allow the dog to turn his head just a little in each direction; over time, he will develop a greater degree of mobility in his neck.

Both versions require a good sit and wait, so you may want to brush up on this before you get started.

Basic option

The trick

For this version of the trick the handler is positioned behind the dog. The dog turns to look back at the handler over his left shoulder, and over his right shoulder.

▶ **Step 1:** This trick relies on the dog responding to a cue to look at you, no matter where he is, so the first stage is to work on his "watch" command. Position the dog facing you, and hold your hands underneath your chin. When the dog looks up to your face, reward him with a treat from your hand. After a few repetitions, the dog should start to look up at you; when he does, give the command "watch" and then reward.

Position yourself behind the dog so that he looks back at you over his left and right shoulders.

First teach the dog to "watch", focusing on your face.

▶ **Step 2:** As your dog's "watch" command becomes more reliable, start to fade the physical cue and hold your hands by your sides rather than under your chin. If the dog looks down at your hands, don't keep repeating your verbal cue. Wait for the dog to give you eye contact and then click, or use your clicker word, bringing your hand, holding a treat, up to your chin before rewarding him. Taking the reward to your chin before rewarding helps the dog to focus on your face again, rather than the hand, or pocket, where the reward came from.

Ask the dog to "watch" with your hands by your sides.

Re-position your hands below your chin before rewarding, to cement the dog's focus on your face.

Focus and Thinking

▶ **Step 3:** Now that the dog will look at you readily, on cue, it's time to check that he can stay in the sit when you position yourself behind him. You may need to go back and reward him, several times, for staying put. Mix up what you are asking for and, sometimes, just take a take a pace backwards and then return to him to reward, in order to build his confidence in staying there.

▶ **Step 4:** Once the dog is reliable in the sit and wait when you are behind him, you can introduce your "watch" cue. Position yourself a few paces behind the dog, then use your upper body to lean to the right, as if you were looking round a corner, and ask the dog to "watch". The dog should turn his head to look at you. If he does, click, or say your clicker word, and return back to his side to reward. Repeat, this time leaning to the left, which should encourage the dog to turn his head to the left. This trick looks extra special if the dog turns his head and then looks down a bit. You can encourage this by lowering your hands, or your body, so the dog really appears to be looking over his shoulder.

Cue the dog to "wait" when you walk behind him.   Lean to the right, and ask him to "watch".   Repeat, this time leaning to the left.

▶ **Step 5:** Gradually, step back further behind the dog while asking him to "watch". However, make sure you always go back to reward him, otherwise he may anticipate and try to come forward, thus turning his body around.

▶ **Step 6:** To make this trick look even more impressive, rather than facing the dog, turn your back on him so you are both facing opposite ways. This way, you will both be turning back to look at each other!

Progresssion

Stand with your back to the dog, and then ask him to "watch".

Advanced option

The trick

For this version of the trick the dog sits facing you and, when asked, looks behind, over his shoulder. This is a lot harder for the dog as he has to look away from the handler, unlike the basic option where he focuses on the handler when asked to "watch". You can work on the advanced version without teaching the basic version first, as the advanced option requires the dog to focus on an object.

The dog looks behind, over his shoulder, on cue.

▶ **Step 1:** To teach this trick, you will need something to use as a point of focus – this could be a toy, a pot of food or a target stick. For the purpose of this exercise, I will use a toy.

Start with the dog sitting facing you, and place the toy between the two of you. Watch closely, and when the dog looks at the toy, click, or use your clicker word, and reward. If you are using a toy as the point of focus, in the early days don't always release the dog to the toy on the floor. Produce another toy as the reward instead.

After a few repetitions, he should start to focus on the toy. At this point, start to move it round towards his left side. As he is fixated on the toy, he should turn his head to the left. When this behaviour is becoming reliable, introduce the "left" command when he moves his head to look at the toy.

When the dog has been marked and reinforced for looking at a toy in front of him, start to move it to his left side.

▶ **Step 2:** The dog should now focus on the toy almost as soon as it is placed. This time place it to the dog's left side, at least a metre (3ft) from where he is sitting. As the dog gets the hang of looking at the toy, start to move it a bit further back – but still at the same distance.

When the dog has been marked and reinforced for looking at a toy in front of him, start to move it to his left side.

▶ **Step 3:** Gradually move the toy so that it's still off to the side, but is further behind the dog. As the toy is placed further behind, he should start looking behind, over his left shoulder. In order to achieve this you will need to work out exactly where to place the toy, which will be dependent on the size of your dog's head and the length of his neck.

Gradually move the toy until it is further behind the dog.

When the toy is placed directly behind the dog, he will need to look over his shoulder in order to see it.

▶ **Step 4:** This is possibly the hardest stage as you need to fade the physical cue of the toy and ask your dog to perform the trick solely on a verbal cue. To do this, start the training session by asking him to perform the move a couple of times with the toy in place, and then discreetly remove it. When you ask for the trick a third time, the dog should look to where the toy was formerly positioned. Watch closely – and be quick to mark with a click, or your clicker word, and reward.

Practise the trick once more, but this time put the toy back in place before you set up the dog for the exercise. In this way he will get a confidence boost when you ask for the move. In the early stages of learning, if you work on too many repitions without the toy in place, the dog will not commit to turning his head. So, therefore it is important to place, and remove, the toy on a random basis.

▶ **Step 5:** Now you have taught the dog to turn his head to the left, you can use the same method and train him to turn his head to the right when giving the dog the "right" command.

▶ **Step 6:** In order for this move to look good, it's not only the turn of the dog's head that is important but also the duration of the dog staying in position. So in order to advance this trick, build up the time period that the dog will hold his head to the left, or right. The best way of doing this is to randomise what you are asking for, so you are rewarding the dog for holding position for both longer and shorter periods.

90   SPORTS DOG, NEW TRICKS

HEAD IN CONE

The trick

This is a useful trick for encouraging focus and independent thinking as the dog has to work out what to do. It is a lovely move to teach if your dog has limited mobility, as all he has to do is place his head in a cone.

The dog places his head in a cone.

I use a plastic cone; the opening needs to be wide enough to accommodate the dog's head. Obviously this will depend on individual conformation, but larger is always better as it will be less intimidating for the dog when he first starts work on the trick. If you don't have a cone, you can teach the trick using a small box – or a top hat if you have one to hand!

▶ **Step 1:** First, hold the cone by the edge in one hand, and let the dog sniff it and investigate it. You may find he looks inside of his own accord, in which case you can click, or use your clicker word, and reward him. If the dog is not readily looking in the cone, place a treat inside, at the bottom of it. The dog should sniff the food and, as soon as he attempts to get his nose inside the cone, mark the behaviour and reward. It may help if you tip the cone so that the dog can get his reward from inside. Bear in mind, at this stage, the dog's head need not go right inside the cone to earn a reward. The aim is to build his confidence.

First let the dog investigate the cone.

Drop a treat into the cone.

▶ **Step 2:** Now that the dog is going into the cone to find food, you want to start shaping the trick so that he is going into the cone without using a treat to bribe him. If you have established the behaviour in step 1, the dog will put his head in the cone and start to investigate the moment it is presented. Mark this with a click, or your clicker word, and reward. This will get the dog thinking that when he puts his head in the cone, he will get a reward from you.

At this stage you may need to reward any attempts, even if the dog's head is not all the way inside. Remember, small steps mean you will get to the end goal quicker. When the behaviour is becoming reliable, introduce the verbal cue, "hat".

The dog will now be anticipating the whereabouts of the treat and should put his head in the cone when you present it.

When you start to fade the food lure, go back to rewarding small steps of progress..

▶ **Step 3:** Now that the dog will place his head in the cone, you can start to build duration. To do this you need to withhold your click, or clicker word, so that the dog tries a little harder. Wait until he holds his head in position just a moment longer, then mark and reward. Again, it is important not to be too greedy when extending the time period. You may have to juggle the rewards between shorter and longer periods otherwise the dog's motivation to perform the move will diminish.

Now work on building duration.

▶ **Step 4:** Up to this point, you will have been holding the cone. To progress the trick, ask the dog to place his head in the cone when it is on the ground. To do this, hold the cone lower until, eventually, you are ready to place it on the floor. An impressive add-on is to position the dog in front of you, at a short distance, and place the open end of the cone on the floor towards him. Ask for "hat" and he should move forward, scoop up the cone with his head, and come a short distance towards you. As the cone will, momentarily, cover his face, the dog needs to be very confident about putting his head in the cone before attempting it.

Progression

Ask the dog to put his head in the cone when it is on the ground...

... and then come towards you.

BIG CIRCLE AROUND OBJECTS

The trick

The dog works at a distance, keeping on the outside of a marked circle.

This trick really shows off your training as the end goal is for the dog to run around in a circle on the far side of cones, which are set in a circle. At any time, the dog has the choice of coming into the circle of cones so he has to learn to look for the next cone and stay on the outside.

If you have a herding breed you might think this is easy, as the dog has the in-built ability to run round in a big circle. However, this can lead to the dog running round without processing what he is doing. This is therefore a great trick for encouraging the dog to think about what it is doing as it will need to keep an eye on the cones in order to keep himself on the outside.

▶ **Step 1:** You might think that you need a large space to start working on this trick but, in fact, a standard size room is ample for early training. The most important element is to teach the dog to stay on the outside of the cones. Start by setting out the cones in a circle with no gaps, or as little space as possible, between them. I would use at least eight cones to start with but the more the better, so there will be minimal gaps between them as the circle gets bigger.

Stand in the middle of the circle and encourage the dog to go around the outside by throwing a treat slightly in front of him and, if you have room, slightly away from the cones. Try to avoid moving around the circle, holding out a treat, and luring the dog. If he needs extra help, bring your hand back towards your body before you throw the reward. With practice, he should start to move in the direction you want, in anticipation of the reward being thrown.

Stand in the middle of a small circle of cones and encourage the dog to go round the outside by throwing a treat ahead of him.

▶ **Step 2:** Keep the same set-up as for step 1 but, this time throw the reward further ahead of the dog and try to stand still rather than turn. Now try to throw a treat from each hand. For example, use your right hand and throw one treat off to the right without moving. Then repeat, this time using your left hand and throwing to the left, again without moving. If you have a good aim, the dog should see each treat, one after the other, which will encourage him to keep circling, even if you are stationary. When you see that the dog is flowing round the outside of the cones, you can name the move with a verbal cue – "out".

Use the same set-up but give the dog less help by standing still rather than turning.

▶ **Step 3:** When the dog is proficient at circling the cones, on cue, without additional help, you can move them out a bit. Gradually position the cones so there are gaps in-between, which will make the circle bigger. If the dog attempts to come inside the cones, try to block him and go back to rewarding more frequently. As with any progression in training, you might need to give your dog a little extra help as you have made the trick harder. Work on building your dog's confidence and you should see him bowing out as he gets to a cone so that he stays on the outside edge of it.

Make the circle bigger with a small gap between each cone. Remember to give extra help, at first, when you make the trick harder.

▶ **Step 4:** It is now time to move to a larger area but, bear in mind, you have to revisit some of the early training so that he is confident in a new location. It might be that you go back to step 2 for a few sessions, and then start to move the cones further out.

Gradually increase the size of the circle, making sure you keep reinforcing the behaviour you want.

▶ **Step 5:** When the dog is consistently going around a bigger circle, you can reduce the number of cones, one at a time. When you are rewarding, make sure you either throw the treat out to him, or run to the edge of the circle and reward him there. Never allow the dog to come into the circle, as he might start doing this in anticipation of the reward.

Now start reducing the number of cones.

Focus and Thinking

Move to a new location so you can make the circle even bigger. Remember to reward on the outside of the cones.

▶ **Step 6:** You are now ready to make the trick harder by moving round the opposite way to the dog. To start with, turn the opposite way, on the spot. Then start to walk the opposite way in a small circle, gradually making the circle bigger so you are walking around the inside of the cones, going the opposite way.

Progression

Give the dog his verbal cue – "out" – and then circle the opposite way.

GO HIDE

The trick

This fun trick requires the dog to go and hide behind an object. It is quite demanding, as the dog has to work through a number of stages, processing instructions, to learn the behaviour.

The object you use can be anything from a chair to a dustbin – just look around your home for an object that your dog can stand behind. For the purpose of this exercise, I will use a chair.

The dog hides behind an object of your choice.

In order to teach this trick you will need to start with some target work. The target can be a mat, which needs to be of sufficient size to accommodate the dog's front feet, or you can use a wooden board of similar size. The advantage of using a board is that it is slightly raised from the floor, so it gives a more definitive place for the dog to position his feet, whereas the mat is pretty much flat to the floor.

> **TOP TIP** *Regardless of the type of target you choose, make sure the surface is significantly different from the floor – or grass if you are working outside – in both colour and texture.*

▶ **Step 1:** Place the target on the floor and hold some food in your fist over it. As the dog approaches your hand, he should place one or both feet on the target. When he does, click, or use your clicker word, to mark the placement of his front feet. At this stage, you want to create a good association with the dog going to the target, so don't be too concerned as to whether both his front feet are on it. The aim is to build good foundations, so the more the dog gets rewarded for being on the target, the stronger the pull to the target will be.

Start by luring the dog so that he places his two front paws on a target.

Increase your distance from the target, and take it to different locations.

▶ **Step 2:** The dog should now be approaching the target in response to your hand signal. The next step is to start to withdraw your hand. To do this, place the target and move around it, stopping at different points. The dog will follow you and, as he does, he should accidentally place a paw, or two, on the target. If this happens mark it with a click, or your clicker word, and reward. Now move slightly away from the target and then back to it. The dog should be focusing on the target and be ready to place his front feet on it. Work on a few repetitions and when this behaviour becomes reliable, you can introduce a verbal cue, "target".

Now that the dog will go to the target, start sending him from the left heel position in readiness for sending him around the chair. The dog should go forward and then turn himself to face you while placing his feet on the target.

▶ **Step 3:** Up until this stage you have been working with the target rather than an object that the dog will hide behind. Now that the target work is strong you can place the target to one side of your chosen object – in this case, a chair. It helps if you position the chair against a wall so the dog always goes to the target in the the same direction. Send him from left heel side, as before, so he goes to the target beside the chair and places his feet on it. As the dog becomes more confident about going to the target when it is near the chair, slowly move it round until it is behind the chair.

Now place the target alongside your chosen object – in this case, a chair – and cue "target".

Gradually move the target until it is behind the chair.

Remember to think about where you reward the dog. If you allow him to come from behind the chair to get his treat, he might start to hide but come round the side of the chair, anticipating the reward. To stop this happening, feed him through the back of the chair, or go up to him and feed directly behind the chair.

▶ **Step 4:** At this stage you are using the target to direct the dog to the correct location, i.e. behind the chair. To prepare him for the next stage – when you will be dispensing with the target – you need to use his familiar "target" command, but add to it, so it becomes "target hide". Over time your dog will start to anticipate what you are asking him to do. At this point, you can drop the "target" part of the command and just use "hide".

SPORTS DOG, NEW TRICKS

> **TOP TIP** To build the dog's confidence, I recommend that chair/object training for this move takes place in exactly the same location. This should mean that the dog is so familiar with performing the trick in a particular location, he will understand what is required when the verbal cue changes.

▶ **Step 5:** Now it's time to remove the target from behind the chair. Make sure you do one or two repetitions using the target before discreetly removing it. Your dog may go to the location, but be confused that he has not found the target, so you will need to be quick to reward. You might then mix your repetitions: some with the target and some without. Over time, the dog will focus on going behind the chair – which is where he has been rewarded – rather than looking for his target.

The final stage is to dispense with the target.

▶ **Step 6:** In order to progress this trick you could ask the dog to perform another trick when he is behind your chosen object. So he might hide behind and *sit pretty* (page 71) or *take a bow* (see page 51). There are many tricks the dog could perform behind an object, so play around and see what you can teach your dog to do.

Progression

Ask the dog to perform another trick, such as *take a bow*, when he is hiding behind the chair.

PLAY DEAD

The trick

As the name of the trick suggests, you want your dog to roll on to his back and place his feet in the air. You can signal it by pointing your fingers at the dog, as if shooting him, which gives the trick added effect when showing it off.

This can be a difficult trick for some dogs as they feel insecure about showing their stomach, so take each step gradually.

The handler 'shoots' and the dog plays dead.

▶ **Step 1:** To ensure this is a positive experience for the dog, train on a soft surface, such as carpet. As you don't want him to roll all the way over, it's a good idea to have a soft object on one side of the dog – a sofa or a big cushion, for example.

To start, ask the dog to go into in the down position, facing you, and then try to get him to flop on to one back leg so that he is in a more relaxed position. If the sofa/cushion is on your left side, you want the dog's left back

The start position.

leg out to the side so it is resting on his right hip. Some dogs find this easier, or more natural, than others, so you may need to spend time rewarding the dog for going into a relaxed down.

▶ **Step 2:** When the dog is in position, hold a treat in your right hand, and lure his head in an anti-clockwise direction over his back. Do not insist that he rolls on to his back. At this stage, you might just need to reward the dog for turning his head over his back. As he finds this rewarding, he will try a little harder and may start to roll on to his back.

Mark and reward the dog for going on to his back, then encourage him to roll back the way he went into the position. So if you took the dog's head anti-clockwise to get him into the position, take his head clockwise to get him back into the down position. The sofa/cushion on your left side will help prevent him rolling right over. It will also encourage him to roll back in a clockwise direction, as it is blocking the anti-clockwise option.

Holding a treat in your right hand, lure the dog's head to turn in an anti-clockwise direction.

Reward progressively so he is encouraged to roll over on his back.

▶ **Step 3:** When the dog is readily following the food and rolling on to his back, you want to concentrate on getting the back of his head on to the floor. Watch closely and be quick to mark and reward when his head is in the correct position. At this stage, don't worry if you get the dog's head in the right position, but the back end hasn't moved – this will occur naturally as the dog becomes more confident.

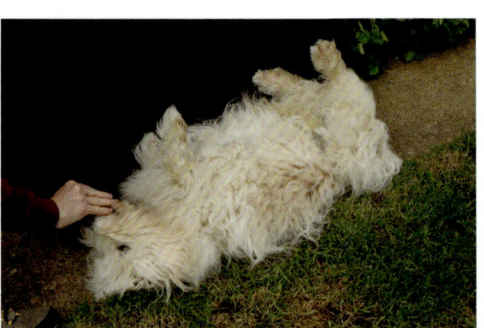

Now work on getting the back of his head on the ground.

▶ **Step 4:** If the dog is consistently rolling on to his back, you can name the trick – "bang". Make sure you only give the verbal cue when the back of his head is on the floor.

Now that the dog is following the food into the position, it's time to remove it. To do this use the hand, without food, to encourage him into position and reward from the other hand. Gradually keep the signal hand higher in order to remove the visual cue.

▶ **Step 5:** Start to move away from the sofa/cushion on your left so that the dog starts to get used to balancing on his back without added support. You also need to build up the time he stays on his back. To do this, take the dog into the position with the food in your fist. When he has the back of his head on the floor, wait a second or two before opening your fist to feed him, and then release him. When the dog goes into the 'dead' position you can also try raising your hand, and then lowering it nearer to him, so that he gets used to going into position when your hand is held higher.

▶ **Step 6:** Now you want to move towards standing up when you ask for "bang". If the dog is struggling with this change in posture, you may need to lean forward to start with, and then gradually stand up straighter.

▶ **Step 7:** If you want to progress this move you can start the dog further away from you before asking him to go into the play dead position. A more advanced sequence using this move would be for the dog to perform it from a sit rather than a down. When the dog collapses into the play dead position from a sit, the trick will look more dramatic!

When the move is on a verbal cue, you can progress to standing up and then adding distance.

Chapter 8
Low Impact Tricks

There will be times, and situations, in your dog's life when he cannot be expected to race around. This could be for any of the following reasons:

- You have restricted training space.
- Your dog is recovering from injury or surgery.
- You have an older dog, with mobility issues, who needs mental stimulation.

Bearing this in mind, I have developed a series of low impact tricks where the dog is either static or only needs to move slowly. For the most part, they involve one part of the body, so you can select tricks that are best suited to your dog's physical capabilities. However, before starting work, your dog should be checked by a health professional and you should discuss the exercises you have in mind.

Some of the low impact tricks are a progression of moves I have already outlined. If this is the case, you may need to revisit the training that is involved in order to brush up your technique and then develop the new move.

FEET ON FEET

The trick

This trick follows on from *middle* (see page 29) where the dog comes in from the right and turns in a clockwise direction to stand between the handler's legs. The dog must be comfortable standing in this position before you start training him to place his front feet on to your feet. You can proceed without teaching him to touch your foot with his paw, but it may help if he nails this first.

If you have small feet the dog will not have much of a target so, in the early days, you will need to make your feet bigger. You can borrow some size 12 shoes or, alternatively, you can make extensions from blocks of wood. If you choose the DIY option, you need to position each block just in front of your toes and, if you can, just underneath your toes, so it makes your feet wider and longer.

The dog comes into the middle position and places his front paws on your feet.

Low Impact Tricks

▶ **Step 1:** Stand with your dog in the middle position and point your toes so they are facing towards each other; in essence, standing 'pigeon toed'.

▶ **Step 2:** Hold the food level with the dog's head and encourage him to move very slightly forward. You may find he walks on to one of your feet accidentally. If this happens, instantly mark and reward. At this stage you are working on getting just one paw on to one of your feet so don't be overly ambitious and ask for both paws, on both feet, too soon.

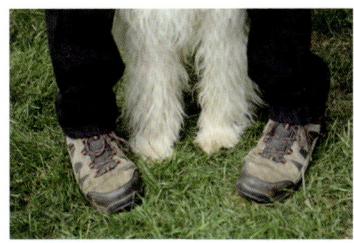

The start position.

> **TOP TIP** *If the dog fails to make any contact with your feet, you will need to give him some help. Do this by placing your toes behind the dog's foot. This should encourage him to lift a paw, and then step back on to your foot. Observe closely and be quick to mark and reward the desired behaviour.*

If the dog accidentally places a paw on one of your feet, be quick to mark and reward.

Some dogs need to be physically shown what to do. If this is the case, and your dog is happy to be handled, you can lift his front leg above the elbow so that the leg stays straight. Then place it down on to your foot and reward.

It may be that your dog responds better if you handle him into position and then reward.

▶ **Step 3:** When the dog is comfortable with placing one paw on one foot, you can work on him doing the same with the other foot.

▶ **Step 4:** The dog should now have an awareness of where to put his paws and should start to feel around for your feet when he comes into the middle position. To help get his paws in the correct place, use the food as a lure and turn the dog's head slightly away from the foot that you want him to target. This will encourage him to weight shift in the same direction as his head is turning, which will mean that the paw you want him to lift becomes lighter. At this stage it is really important that your feet are super-size and the dog has plenty of space to place his feet.

Turn the dog's head away from the foot you want him to target.

▶ **Step 5:** When the dog is consistently coming between your legs and trying to position his paws on your feet, you can introduce a verbal cue, "toes".

▶ **Step 6:** You will, probably, have been bending forward to help the dog position his paws so now try to stand straighter. When the dog feels comfortable in position, raise your hands – which have been signalling/luring him – for a brief moment before returning them. Gradually hold your hands higher as the dog comes between your legs so that he no longer needs them as a physical cue to encourage him to get on your feet and stay in position.

Briefly raise your hands so he maintains position without your help.

▶ **Step 7:** Up until this stage you have been standing still, so now you are going to attempt to walk! Start by flexing your toes so that the dog gets used to some movement under his paws while you are standing still. Then start to lift your toes slightly off the floor. Initially, you may need to hold the reward close to the dog's nose so that he doesn't retract a paw. You will need to build his confidence gradually, until you are able to lift your foot slightly off the ground. How much you can raise your foot will depend on your dog's ability to bend his leg, so you might be better to shuffle along rather than take big steps.

▶ **Step 8:** Start to take a few small steps forward, rewarding the dog frequently to build confidence. As he gets used to movement you can again stand up straighter, and remove your hands.

Progression

Work at performing this trick on the move!

WRAP A LEG AROUND A CANE

The trick

For this trick the dog places his wrist around a cane, which the handler holds in a vertical position. To perform the move, you must first teach your dog to *give a paw* (see page 33). You might also need work on desensitizing your dog to the cane, as some dogs can be fearful of this type of object.

▶ **Step 1:** When you have reviewed your dog's paw to hand touch, position him so that he is sitting facing you. The cane should be in your right hand, with the other end resting on the floor. Make sure you keep a firm grip on it as it as you don't want it to slip and slide when the dog puts his paw on it. Initially the cane should be held

The dog wraps his wrist around a cane, which you are holding.

diagonally across the front of the dog, which will encourage him to rest his wrist/leg over it. As the dog grows in confidence, and understands what is required, you can, gradually, move the cane until it is in a vertical position.

▶ **Step 2:** Hold your left hand out, above the cane, and ask the dog to touch it with his paw. At this stage, the dog is not resting his paw on the cane, he is simply getting into the habit of placing his leg over the cane. Repeat, but this time hold your left hand closer to your body so the dog has to reach over the cane to touch it. You want him to place his wrist – not his paw – over the cane. To encourage this, ask him to give a paw but hold your left hand lower down so he has to reach even further forward with his paw.

Position the cane on a diagonal line, hold out your left hand and ask the dog to hand touch with his right paw.

▶ **Step 3:** When the dog is reaching over the cane to touch your left hand, start to hold it so that it is just out of touching range. The dog will then retract his paw, and you should find his wrist brushes the cane or rests on it fleetingly. At this exact point, you need to be ready to mark the behaviour with a click, or your clicker word, and reward. When the dog is consistently performing the move, you can start to add the command, "wrap".

Hold your hand closer to your body so the dog has to reach over the cane to touch it.

▶ **Step 4:** The dog should now be comfortable sitting and placing his wrist over the cane, which is positioned diagonally across his front. You may find that the dog is actually pulling the cane slightly towards him with his wrist; this is a good indicator that you can gradually move the cane to a more vertical position. Over the next few sessions gradually take the cane from the diagonal to the vertical position, making sure the dog is comfortable at each stage, as his wrist placement will change.

Low Impact Tricks

When the dog is starting to rest his wrist on the cane, start to move it to a more vertical position.

Now stand up and ask for the move.

At this stage, you need to consider how you are going to hold the top of the cane: alongside the dog's head on the side that he is wrapping the cane, or on the opposite side. Most dogs have a natural preference, so always go with what your dog favours. When you have taught him to wrap one leg around the cane, you can go back to step 1 and repeat for the other leg.

▶ **Step 5:** To make this trick more impressive, position the dog on your left-hand side and ask him to wrap his paw around the cane while you do the same – one leg crossing the other. If you want to advance this move further you can send the dog to a post that is situated at a distance and ask him to wrap his paw around it.

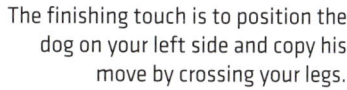

The finishing touch is to position the dog on your left side and copy his move by crossing your legs.

Progression

Teach the dog to wrap a cane with his left leg.

Take yourself out of the process so the dog learns to wrap his leg around a cane independently.

REMOVING CARDS FROM SLOTS

The trick

This is a lovely, relatively static, trick to teach your dog if he has limited mobility. The end goal is for the dog to pull out a series of playing cards, which are placed in slots, starting at the top and working downwards. You will need to construct a holder for the playing cards, which can be made of wood or cardboard, and you will also need a plentiful supply of cardboard cut-out cards before moving on to playing cards.

The dog pulls cards from slots, working from top to bottom.

▶ **Step 1:** Ask the dog to sit in front of you, and hold out a cardboard card as if it is in a slot. If the dog goes to smell or nibble it, click, or say your clicker word, and reward. As you keep rewarding the dog for showing interest in the card, he should start to use his front teeth a little more. At some stage, he will take a hold of the card and probably pull it slightly. This is when you should let go of the card.

As the dog becomes more proficient, keep hold of the card marginally longer as he may need to use a bit more pull when the card is in a slot. You are now ready to name the behaviour with a "pull" command.

Hold out a card and progressively reward the dog for showing an interest in it, and then taking it in his mouth.

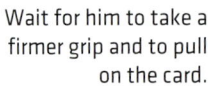

Wait for him to take a firmer grip and to pull on the card.

Low Impact Tricks   109

When your dog is confidently taking hold of the cardboard card introduce him to the smaller, thinner playing card. This will feel different, so you might need to revisit your earlier training. However, it will take no time before the dog is accustomed to taking a playing card from you.

▶ **Step 2:** The next stage is for the dog to pull the card from the slot rather than your hand. To do this, it may be helpful to make a small cardboard holder, with one slot, so as not to confuse the dog by having a big board in front of him. Now follow the same procedure as you did earlier when holding the card – but this time the card is in a slot.

Now transfer the behaviour so the dog pulls the card from a slot. To avoid confusion, use a single card.

▶ **Step 3:** When you are ready, bring out the big board. The aim is for the dog to pull the cards out from the top and then go down to the next and so on – but you will need to move on to this by degrees. Start by spacing two cards out, one at the top and one a bit further down. Help the dog by indicating the top card first. Initially you might need to reward him, every time, for pulling out the top card until he fully understands that this is his starting point.

▶ **Step 4:** Bring the two cards a little closer together and, when the dog is reliably removing these in sequence, you can progress to placing more cards in slots. You can advance this trick by positioning the cardholder at a distance, and then sending the dog to perform the trick. You can also work on giving the dog a single verbal cue – "pull" –to remove all the cards, rather than giving multiple commands every time you want another card removed.

You are now ready to add more cards, and to teach the dog to remove them in order, working from top to bottom.

CLOSE A DRAWER

The trick

This is a fun trick that requires the dog to use his nose to close a drawer back into a cupboard. The principle element of this trick is teaching the dog to push with his nose. This is a highly transferrable skill, so once he has learnt this, you can direct it to different objects, such as pressing a button or pushing a football along.

The dog uses his nose to close a drawer.

▶ **Step 1:** To start this trick, review the training for a *hand touch* (see page 25). Make sure you work on duration – the time the dog will keep his nose on your hand – as this will help when it comes to pushing a drawer.

▶ **Step 2:** Now stick a small label on the palm of your hand and ask the dog to "touch". This is the first stage of teaching the dog to transfer his nose touch to another object. Work on duration. Then start to move your hand away from the dog as he touches it, replicating a drawer being pushed into a cupboard. The aim is for the dog to maintain contact with your hand as you move it.

Stick a label to the palm of your hand.

Ask the dog to "touch" and, progressively, work on duration.

▶ **Step 3:** Once the dog is keeping his nose pressed to the label when you move your hand, you are ready to transfer it to your chosen object; in this case, a drawer. Start by sticking the label on the drawer and point to it, asking the dog to "touch". At this stage you don't want the drawer to move, as that might shock the dog, so make sure it is pushed into the cupboard. Work on asking the dog to "touch" the sticky label, and rewarding, until he is volunteering to go to it without the help of a hand signal.

▶ **Step 4:** Now stand behind the drawer and open it just a fraction. If possible, position yourself behind the drawer; this will be easier for the dog, as he is pushing the drawer towards you. If you have to stand beside the dog, make sure you reward him close to the drawer when he touches the label. This will encourage him to keep his nose close to the drawer. Initially reward any attempt to push the drawer, then gradually refine what you require.

Now stick the label on a closed drawer and ask for "touch".

Work progressively until the drawer is pulled out to a reasonable distance and the dog is confidently pushing it shut. If possible, maintain your position behind the drawer. At this stage it is advisable to switch verbal cues from "touch" to "push" so that the two are not confused. To do this, attach the two commands "touch-push" then, in time, reduce it to "push".

Gradually open the drawer and the dog will learn to apply more pressure so he can close the drawer.

▶ **Step 5:** Now it's time to phase out the label that you have stuck on the drawer. There are two ways of doing this. The first option is to, gradually, reduce the size of the label. Alternatively, you can ask for a nose touch on the label, reward while removing it, and then quickly ask for another nose touch. As the dog has been rewarded for this behaviour, he will, more than likely, repeat it without thinking. However, you will need to replace the label for the next repetition to reinforce that this is what you want.

▶ **Step 6:** It is harder for the dog to go forward from your side and push the drawer shut, so work towards moving further away from the drawer before sending the dog.

Once the dog has perfected this trick, you can start to experiment in other scenarios, such as shutting a door.

The last stage is to phase out the label.

FLIP AND THROUGH A HULA HOOP

The trick

This trick is motivational, but it is not too strenuous, and suits dogs of all sizes. The aim is for the dog to use his nose to flip under the edge of the hoop and then continue through it. The only equipment you need is a hoop that is of sufficient size to allow your dog to go through it comfortably.

▶ **Step 1:** Hold the hoop in your left hand, and position the dog on your left side, holding the hoop in front of him. With a treat in your right hand, encourage the dog to go through the hoop. Gradually lower the top of the hoop towards the dog so he has to duck a bit before he goes through it. As you position the hoop closer to the floor, he will start to feel it on his back as he goes through, so be quick to reward so he maintains motivation. When rewarding, either throw the treat, on or make sure the dog has emerged from the hoop.

The dog uses his nose to flip a hoop and then go through it.

Hold the hoop in your left hand and, using a treat in your right hand, encourage the dog to go through it.

Gradually lower the hoop so the dog has to duck to go through it.

▶ **Step 2:** The next stage is to get the dog to use the top of his nose to flip the hoop. As before, hold the hoop close to the ground but, this time, hold the treat below the edge of the hoop. This should encourage the dog to go down and push under

Low Impact Tricks   113

the edge with his nose. The moment he does this, mark with a click, or your clicker word, and reward. Gradually lower the hoop edge until the dog starts to really push his nose under it. At this stage you can introduce your verbal cue, "hoop".

Now encourage the dog to walk through after he has raised the hoop edge. Initially you might want to give him some help by holding the hoop so it is only just touches his back.

Up until now you have held the hoop with your left hand. The next stage is to balance it on you foot rather than holding it. Make sure there is still a gap between the floor and the hoop so that the dog can get his nose underneath.

To teach him to flip the hoop, hold the treat below the edge of it.

When the dog has raised the hoop, encourage him to walk through it.

▶ **Step 3:** Now you need to remove the lure of the food. To do this, rest the hoop on your foot, and hold your right hand low down near the floor, so it is in place to help the dog if he is struggling. Ideally you want the dog to go down with his nose first. If he does, click, or use your clicker word, and reward from the left hand. If he works out what you want after the first few repetitions, you are on a fast track to standing up and withdrawing your hand completely.

▶ **Step 4:** The last stage is for the dog to flip the hoop while it lies flat on the floor. Obviously, this will be much harder if you are working on a slippery floor surface and, equally, not all breeds have sufficient length of muzzle to get the right angle to flip the hoop. In both these scenarios, you will need to help by keeping the hoop edge slightly raised.

Once the dog can perform this trick with ease, you can progress it by sending him from a distance to flip the hoop.

Finally, ask the dog to flip the hoop, without your help, while it is lying flat on the floor.

NODDING DOG

The trick

This is a cute trick in which the dog nods his head up and down. Again, it requires minimal movement, but the dog will still need to use his brain! It will help if he has already learnt the skill of nose touching an object, (see *close a drawer,* page 110).

Before starting to teach the trick, you need a stool, or a box, which is about half the height of the dog. For the purposes of this exercise, I will refer to a box. You will also need a lid from a food container, preferably a different colour from the box/stool.

▶ **Step 1:** The first step is to get the dog to nose touch the lid from the food container. If you have already taught him to close a drawer you should find that it only takes a few repetitions before he is nose touching the lid while you hold it in your hand. When the dog is readily touching it, hold it so it is below the height of his head. Introduce different heights – both easier and harder – so that he doesn't lose confidence.

▶ **Step 2:** Position the dog, in a sit, in front of the box and place the lid on the top of it, close to the dog.

Note: if have taught **pirouette on a box** *(see page 48), you might want to use a different object – a stool, for example, which the dog will not associate with this move.*

Position your hand close to the lid, and ask the dog to nose "touch". Work on this until you can stand up straight, and the dog can take his nose down to the lid. Every time he touches the lid, click, or use your clicker word, and reward. For this trick, you don't need duration, so you can reward him any time he touches the lid.

The dog nods his head up and down.

First hold a target in your hand and reward the dog for nose-touching it.

At this point it is advisable to introduce a command to name the nodding motion rather than repeating "touch". The best way to do this is to use a cue that bridges the two behaviours – " touch-nod". When the dog has responded correctly to this, over a few sessions, drop in the occasional "nod" command. Eventually you can just use "nod" as the verbal cue for this trick.

Transfer the target to a box and ask the dog to "touch".

▶ **Step 3:** Replace the box with something lower, so that the dog gets used to lowering his head further in order to touch the lid. When he becomes proficient, place the lid on the floor. As you want a nodding motion, you may find that you need to reward the dog when his head comes up to look at you, rather than when it is down near the lid.

Transfer the target to a box and ask the dog to "touch".

Now place the target on the ground, and, over time, randomise whether it is present or not.

▶ **Step 4:** The last stage is to remove the lid target and, in order to do this, you need to perform a little bit of disappearing magic!

Start by placing the lid on the ground, reward a couple repetitions, then discreetly remove the lid and quickly ask for "nod". As the dog has just done two repetitions of this behaviour, he should automatically lower his head to touch the spot where the lid was located.

Initially he may be a bit baffled as to the whereabouts of the lid, so make sure you mark any downwards movement of the head – even if his nose doesn't touch the floor. As you are rewarding this first attempt, replace the lid and ask for the trick again. As the lid is in position, the dog should perform the trick correctly.

Now all you need to do is randomise whether the lid is present, or not. In this way, the dog will, over time, gain confidence and will perform the trick without the lid serving as a visual prompt.

▶ **Step 5:** To smarten up the trick you need the dog to do at least two or three nods when you ask for it. To get these three nods on a single command, re-introduce the lid and give your verbal cue. When the dog responds to "nod", withhold the reward and wait for him to process what he should do to earn a treat. The likelihood is that he will try the 'nod' move again. If he opts for this, give him lots of praise and a jackpot reward. In this way, he will learn that he has to do the move multiple times before he gains a reward.

The dog will be used to you standing nearby as he performs the trick so, when he is fully confident, you can increase the degree of difficulty by gradually standing further away from him.

DIG

The trick

This trick requires the dog to dig – a behaviour that comes naturally to many dogs. However, you are asking for something extra as, most likely, you will be inside, teaching your dog to dig on a hard surface rather than digging in soft earth, which would be his preference. Also,

The dog 'digs' on cue – even though you may be asking for this move on a hard surface.

soil will readily move which stimulates the dog to keep digging, but when this trick is perfected you will be asking your dog to dig no matter the surface.

To teach this move, you will need an old towel. As the towel needs to decrease in size as the trick progresses, make sure it's one which you don't mind cutting up.

▶ **Step 1:** Position the dog in front of you, then kneel down and hold part of the towel with your left hand. Place some food in your right hand and put it under the towel, close to the dog and the edge of the towel. There are two ways to proceed, depending on how much help the dog needs:

Option 1: Leave a treat under the towel, and any attempt at pawing will be rewarded by revealing the food. If you go for this option, mix up allowing the dog to get the treat from under the towel and rewarding him from your hand, above the towel. This is because you don't want your dog to get fixated on going under the towel to get the food. If you randomly reward above the towel, it will help him to realise that he must do something extra, rather than relying on finding food under the towel.

Place some food under a towel. When the dog paws at the towel it will reveal the treat.

Option 2: If your dog needs more help, you can hold a treat in your fist and poke it under the edge of the towel, withdraw it, and then poke it back under, which will encourage him to scrape at the towel. Reward any attempt at pawing by revealing the food in your hand, under the towel.

Alternatively, hold a treat under the towel, which will encourage the dog to scrape at it – and then be rewarded.

Keep training sessions short, and reward thick and fast to maintain motivation. If the dog is not excited at the prospect of finding food, or he requires too many attempts before being rewarded, he will start to go on strike.

▶ **Step 2:** After a few sessions, producing the towel and/or poking your hand under it will prompt the dog to start scratching. If he is digging with one, or two, paws, at this stage, you can introduce a command, "dig-dig" as he is performing the move. Now progress to holding one hand, then the other, away from the towel until you can see that the dog is performing the dig on the towel and not because your hand is low down, under, or near, the towel.

> **TOP TIP** *When you are starting to phase out your hands, place your knee or foot on the towel so the dog can get a good purchase, which will encourage him to repeat the "dig-dig" behaviour.*

▶ **Step 3:** Start to decrease the size of the towel. As you do this, start looking for those moments when the dog goes to dig – but misses – and digs on the floor rather than the towel. When this happens go mad with the praise, as getting him to dig on a surface, without the prompt of the towel, is the next progression. At this stage, mix between making the towel more, and less, obvious to boost the dog's confidence.

▶ **Step 4:** Phasing out the towel will probably take many weeks. You may think your dog has mastered the move without the towel but, perhaps due to different flooring or other distractions he is unsure, so you will have to bring in the towel again to cement his learning.

▶ **Step 5:** Until this point you will have been working at floor level so now you need to start to stand up and phase out any hand signals that may have crept in, such as pointing at the floor.

Gradually decrease the size of the towel and be ready to mark those moments when the dog digs on the ground rather than the towel.

The final stage is to stand upright – and to phase out the towel.

Once you have got dig on cue, you could advance it by attaching it to another trick, such as *go hide* (see page 95). This would entail sending the dog behind an object, and then asking him to dig. This is a big progression, as the dog has to perform the dig without being able to see you.

Summary

Hopefully you have worked through many of the tricks in this book and have had some fun – and even some laughter – while trying to perfect them!

As I have highlighted throughout this book, there are many benefits to be gained from trick training in terms of your dog's physical fitness and mental development. However, training is a team effort and, you, the handler, are an important part of the equation.

When you are working on a trick, take time to analyse your training sessions and you will gain valuable information that may be directly applicable to your chosen discipline.

Consider the following:

What went well, and why?

- What struggles did you encounter, and why did these issues arise?
- Was there something you did, or failed to do, which hindered the learning process.

If you answer these questions honestly, and objectively, you may discover why there are some exercises, or elements of learning, in your chosen sport which your dog finds difficult. Once these issues are identified, you can find ways to improve both your training, and your handling.

When working on the tricks, you should also be on the lookout for things that could help in other scenarios. It might be that there are words you use, or a particular tone of voice, that really excites your dog, and this could be transferred to your own sport. Alternatively there may be a trick that your dog really enjoys, which you can use to get his brain into gear before starting the work for your own discipline.

As handlers, we often have a more positive, fun attitude when training tricks as we tend have so much invested in our own chosen sport. We can, therefore, use tricks to lighten the mood, particularly in situations which dogs find stressful. For example, if you turn up at a venue and your dog seems worried and unsure of himself, take the opportunity to run through some of his favourite tricks, which will help him to make a more positive connection with the environment.

Above all, remember that learning tricks is a great downtime from the complexities of some of the dog sports. So when you are working together keep a smile on your face, and convey to your dog that you, too, are having fun learning something new.